Praise for
The Evolution of a Corporate Idealist
and Christine Bader

"Business must be part of the solution to the complex challenges facing our planet. This requires authentic and committed leaders at all levels within a company working together to help make this a reality. In *The Evolution of a Corporate Idealist: When Girl Meets Oil,* Christine Bader gives us a firsthand account of what it takes to get this right and provides some salutary lessons about what it means when companies get it wrong."

—Paul Polman, CEO, Unilever

"Companies increasingly recognize that they have a legitimate interest in respecting human rights. Christine Bader has been on the front lines of both setting and implementing human rights standards for business, and provides an engaging narrative of what it takes to ensure that human rights are a reality for all."

—Mary Robinson, former president of Ireland; former United Nations High Commissioner for Human Rights

"With insight and humor, Christine Bader sheds light on the inner workings of multinational business. *The Evolution of a Corporate Idealist* is a must-read for all of us who care about ensuring that ethics and morality have their rightful place on the business agenda."

—William H. Donaldson, 27th chairman, SEC; former chairman and chief executive, New York Stock Exchange; co-founder, former chairman and CEO, Donaldson, Lufkin & Jenrette

"For all those who have seen what multinational corporations are doing and wondered, 'What were they *thinking*?'—read this book! Bader takes us deep inside big business, past the slick P.R. and newspaper headlines. Whether you resonate with the title "Corporate Idealist" or think it's an oxymoron, this book is a fascinating read. Love Big Oil or hate it, you'll never look at it the same."

—Annie Leonard, Founder, *The Story of Stuff* Project

"Christine Bader writes as she is: genuine, funny, compassionate, on a constant search for truth and impact. *The Evolution of a Corporate Idealist: When Girl Meets Oil* is a unique and valuable contribution to one of the greatest challenges of the modern era: how to leverage the creativity and drive of business to achieve a just and sustainable world."

—Aron Cramer, President and CEO,
BSR (Business for Social Responsibility)

"Too many companies—and the investors and consumers that support them—still take a short-term, narrow view that is threatening our planet; the 'sustainability' movement has often felt like one step forward, two steps back. In *The Evolution of a Corporate Idealist: When Girl Meets Oil*, Christine Bader gives us an insider's perspective on why that is the case. I relate to her struggle between optimism and pessimism, and suspect many others will too."

—Jeffrey Hollender, founder and former
CEO, Seventh Generation

"*The Evolution of a Corporate Idealist* is a deeply personal reflection on a vastly neglected subject: the hopes and successes, disappointments and disillusionments, of corporate social responsibility practitioners in global companies. Christine Bader recounts her own journey, starting with infatuation and fulfillment, to feeling jilted, experimenting with taming capitalism through the United Nations, and ending up back in the private sector, a bit bruised but considerably wiser. This makes for an eminently readable introduction to the burgeoning field of corporate social responsibility."

—John G. Ruggie, Harvard University; former United
Nations special representative for business & human rights

"Girl meets Big Oil, Big Oil breaks girl's heart. So far, so predictable. But Christine Bader's extraordinary, warts-and-all memoir reveals what happens when idealism and business converge in both the heart and the mind."

—John Elkington, co-founder of Environmental Data Services (ENDS), SustainAbility and Volans; co-author, *The Power of Unreasonable People*

"Christine Bader's *The Evolution of a Corporate Idealist* paints a vivid picture of the changing world of business, the rise of sustainability as a value in many companies, and the author's own awakening to the complexity of corporate responsibility. Written as a lively and compelling narrative, the book goes beyond recounting Bader's ups and downs in a decade at BP to offer deep insight into the central importance of morality in any job, company, or life."

—Dan Esty, Hillhouse Professor, Yale University; author, *Green to Gold*

THE
EVOLUTION
OF A
CORPORATE
IDEALIST

THE EVOLUTION OF A CORPORATE IDEALIST

WHEN GIRL MEETS OIL

CHRISTINE BADER

First published by Bibliomotion, Inc.
39 Harvard Street
Brookline, MA 02445
617-934-2427
www.bibliomotion.com

Printed in the United States of America

Library of Congress Cataloging-in-Publication Data

Bader, Christine.
    The evolution of a corporate idealist : when girl meets oil / Christine Bader.
        pages cm
    Summary: "The Evolution of a Corporate Idealist is based on Bader's experience with BP and then with a United Nations effort to prevent and address human rights abuses linked to business"— Provided by publisher.
    ISBN 978-1-937134-88-4 (hardback) — ISBN 978-1-937134-89-1 (ebook) — ISBN 978-1-937134-90-7 (enhanced ebook)
    1. Bader, Christine. 2. BP (Firm)—Social aspects. 3. Petroleum industry and trade—Social aspects. 4. Social responsibility of business. 5. Human rights. I. Title.
    HD9571.9.B73B33 2014
    338.7'6655092—dc23
                          2013046545

To A & C & A

Contents

*A good business should be both competitively successful
and a force for good.*

—BP, "What We Stand For,"
Statement of Business Policies, 2002

*There is a great deal of difference in believing something still,
and believing it again.*

—W.H. Auden

Prologue

NEW HAVEN: GIRL MEETS OIL

Big Oil and I got together in the summer of 1999. It all started a few months earlier, in a packed lecture hall in New Haven, Connecticut.

John Browne, chief executive of what was then British Petroleum, came to deliver a speech about his ambitious plans to reduce the company's greenhouse gas emissions. He had recently broken ranks with his oil titan peers to become the first head of a major energy company to acknowledge the reality of climate change and urge action.

I was a first-year MBA student at Yale, wondering whether I would find inspiration in the private sector after years of working in government and nonprofits and observing the power of business from the outside.

After college I did a year of community service with City Year, the AmeriCorps program, and got to know the corporate sponsors who donated money and goods and sent employees out to mentor and serve with us. I was a Teaching Fellow in Community Service at Phillips Academy Andover, organizing students from the well-endowed prep school to work with residents of Lawrence, a bustling textile producer in the late 1800s that had become one of the poorest cities in Massachusetts. I worked in the New York City Mayor's Office, where companies were wooed for their jobs and tax revenues.

It dawned on me that while many companies were making positive contributions to society, some of them were simultaneously creating the conditions that necessitated their largesse. The poor neighborhoods I worked in had been devastated by the loss of industry, with their pain then compounded as the tax base dwindled and school quality declined. In some cases, business's negative impacts were much more direct: companies polluted, or lobbied to replace a public garden with a parking lot, or failed to hire anyone from the community they had moved into.

The influence of business intrigued me. Who are these company executives? How and why do they get to decide whether a community thrives or falters?

I had ignored the corporate recruiters on my college campus. My parents both worked "in business," but growing up I had no idea what that meant. Every morning I saw my dad don his suit and my mom wiggle into her nude pantyhose, and both of them leave for the overcrowded New York City subway. After my sister and I had dinner with our babysitter, they would come home exhausted, and I had little understanding of what had happened in the interim.

But as a young adult, I was starting to see the power of the corporate world. I wasn't sure if I wanted any of that power for myself—I thought it might repulse me—but I wanted to see it up close.

I made my way to business school, but without a clear idea of where I would go next. My classmates started throwing their résumés in for investment banking and consulting interviews as soon as we got to campus, but I hoped that something more inspiring would come along.

Then, on that autumn morning, John Browne appeared. "Companies are not separate from the societies in which they work," he said. "We don't make our profits and then go and live somewhere else. This is our society too. The people who work for us are also citizens. They have hopes and fears for themselves and for their families. Companies which want to keep operating successfully on a long-term basis can't isolate themselves from society."

Ten years later this would be standard CEO prose, but at the time Browne's lofty rhetoric was catnip to me. I landed an internship in BP's executive office in London, excited to be there for a few months but unsure whether it would prove anything more than a summer fling.

I was at first pleasantly surprised, then seduced by what I found: a group of clean-cut, well-dressed men (and a few women) who oozed that lovely dry British wit, and who had worked all over the world in different jobs, from hands-on operational roles to finance to government affairs. Most importantly to me, they seemed to be in constant conversation about the company's role in society, whether fighting climate change or supporting the communities where it had operations. I cared about social justice but had no idea people in the private sector did too, and was entranced to hear corporate executives talk this way. I felt like an American exchange student hearing Italian for the first time.

I fell in love with that BP. And BP loved me back, giving me the opportunity to live in Indonesia, working on the social issues around a remote gas field; then China, ensuring worker and community safety for a chemicals joint venture; then in the United Kingdom again, collaborating with colleagues around the world to better understand and support human rights.

BP was paying me to help the people living around its projects, because that in turn would help its business. I was living the cliché of doing well and doing good, and I was completely smitten. My beloved company even let me create a *pro bono* project advising a United Nations initiative to clarify business's responsibilities for human rights, aimed at creating international policy to help even more people.

Then Big Oil broke my heart.

I should have seen it coming. During what would turn out to be the last few years of Browne's tenure as chief executive, BP had a number of terrible accidents, and Browne eventually resigned under a cloud of scandal. Tony Hayward, head of the exploration and production division, took over, deemphasized the progressive stances that Browne had staked out on human rights and renewable energy, and pledged to focus "like a laser on safe and reliable operations"—a commitment that would be betrayed in spectacular fashion. I left BP to work on the U.N. project full-time, but attributed the breakup more to what I was pursuing than what I was leaving: it's not you, it's me.

Then came the Deepwater Horizon explosion and the BP that emerged in the aftermath. My former employer was portrayed not as kind and caring but manipulative and murderous, more Macbeth than Romeo. To believe some of the news and commentary would be to believe that it wasn't all Hayward's fault, that the bad BP had been there all along, hiding in plain sight. The Deepwater Horizon explosion didn't undo the good work I had done in Asia and elsewhere, but I no longer knew what to believe. Had my nine-year relationship with BP been a sham?

I looked for love elsewhere. The U.N. work was good for a while, but the politics and the abstraction didn't suit me. The activists I saw in action struck me as passionate but impractical and relentlessly negative, focusing on what was wrong and what couldn't be, whereas I wanted to imagine what was possible and make it happen.

The more I flirted with others, the more I felt myself drawn back to business. I found the people in multinational corporations idealistic but pragmatic, earnest but self-deprecating, appreciative of the resources but wrestling with the responsibilities. In other words, they were just like me.

And their companies were as flawed and complex as BP, advancing human rights in some ways while compromising them in others. The companies struggling with accelerating globalization, technology, and their evolving role in the world were not just in the industries whose problems have become well-known, namely extractives, for the environmental and social damage where they pull up resources; and footwear and apparel for sweatshops. Joining the debate were Google, Microsoft, and Yahoo! for involvement in censorship or surveillance; Apple, for sourcing from factories with poor working conditions; and banks, for funding harmful infrastructure projects and undermining the global economy.

Of course, business causing harm isn't new. Slavery was the engine of the U.S. cotton trade until the Civil War. The Triangle Shirtwaist Factory fire in 1911 killed 146 garment workers in New York City. Upton Sinclair's 1906 book *The Jungle* detailed exploitation in the American meatpacking industry.

The same conditions exist today, at home and abroad. The International Labour Organization estimated in 2008 that annual profits generated from human trafficking are as high as $32 billion. A 2005 Human Rights Watch report called *Blood,*

Sweat, and Fear: Workers' Rights in U.S. Meat and Poultry Plants might as well have been written by Sinclair. In 2013, 1,129 garment workers died when the Rana Plaza building collapsed in Bangladesh.

These problems persist despite the growth of corporate social responsibility (CSR) and sustainability, disciplines for which there are now degrees, conferences, magazines, and hashtags. The social responsibility of companies and executives is mentioned in academic literature in the 1930s and '40s. But the concept did not enter the mainstream until the late 1990s, when Nike faced pressure to take greater responsibility for its Asian suppliers' labor practices and Shell was accused of complicity in the execution of Ken Saro-Wiwa, who had been protesting Shell's activities in the Niger Delta.

In 2012, more than half of the companies in the Fortune 500 published CSR or sustainability reports, and many have chief sustainability officers, CSR departments, or some version thereof. Many companies have long had philanthropic foundations, but this new iteration of corporate citizenship is closer to core operations, focusing on how the business earns its money rather than just how to give it away.

I realized that I am part of a global army of people fighting for better social and environmental practices inside multinational companies—with mixed success. I started to see every corporate disaster in the headlines differently. Instead of being mad at a monolithic, faceless corporation, I wondered about the people who were deep in the company, out of public view, pushing for policies and procedures that might have prevented the disaster from occurring. Why did they fail? How did they feel? And who are they—we—anyway?

We are Corporate Idealists. We're in Asia's factory zones, working with local managers to make sure employees are paid and treated properly. We're in Africa, sitting on dirt floors with village elders to protect indigenous traditions amidst an influx of foreign oil workers. We're in Silicon Valley, collaborating with product developers to better protect user privacy. We're in London and New York, convincing our directors that protecting people and the planet is good for business.

We believe that business can be a force for good, even as we struggle with our own contradictions: we don't join antiglobalization protests, but agree with some of their calls for reform. We're disgusted by excessive CEO compensation, but aspire to do better for ourselves and our families. We push our companies to offer sustainable products, but balk at organic prices when doing our own shopping. We defend our companies to investors and campaigners, but insist to our colleagues that we're not doing enough.

We are trying to prevent the next Deepwater Horizon explosion and the next Rana Plaza collapse, playing defense while also moving toward a vision of a better future. Sometimes, obviously, we fail.

We have experienced heartache and disillusionment. But we also know that big business can make the world a better place, and feel compelled to do all we can to make that happen.

Are we delusional or realistic? Are we changing the way that business is done or tinkering at the margins? Terrified of the risks or excited by the opportunities? Is our love of big business justified or misguided?

Yes. This is our story.

⁓

This book recounts my time working with BP in Indonesia, China, and the United Kingdom, then with the United Nations secretary-general's special representative on business and human rights. Along the way I weave in stories and reflections from some of the Corporate Idealists I've gotten to know over the years to show that while my story may be unique in its details, it is not in its themes.

I have reconstructed conversations and events based on my correspondence, documents, research, and memory. I have tried in good faith to check my facts and test my recollections with others, but recognize that memories are fallible and histories subjective. I am grateful to all of the friends, peers, and former colleagues who have been so generous with their time and thoughts, and take responsibility for any errors, misrepresentations, or oversights.

Chapter 1

INDONESIA: ON THE FRONT LINES

Soaked in sweat, I stumbled over tree roots as I tried to keep up with the short, stocky man with the large machete. It was February 2001 and I was in Papua, Indonesia's easternmost province.

We were walking away from the spot where BP, my new employer, was to build a liquefied natural gas (LNG) plant. On the proposed plant site was a village called Tanah Merah, or "red land" in Indonesian, for the rich color of the clay the village stood on. Tanah Merah was home to 127 households that would have to move to new homes that BP would build. I was there to see the new village site for the first time. The man in front of me was Jonas, one of Tanah Merah's leaders.

We trekked inland from the bay that housed the gas, hacking through dense brush, and eventually stopped at a small clearing.

"*Di sini,*" said Jonas. *Here it is.*

We were far from the coast, standing in a patch of dry grass. This was nothing like the village's current location, on open fertile land overlooking the bay—the perfect spot for people who live on the fish and shellfish they catch.

I raised an eyebrow, wondering if the situation seemed as unjust to Jonas as it did to me. Jonas shrugged, seemingly resigned to his fate.

The project was called Tangguh, "strong" or "resilient" in Indonesian. BP would extract the gas from the bay and send it by underwater pipeline to the LNG plant, where it would be chilled to -260 degrees Fahrenheit, condensed for loading into tankers, and shipped around the Pacific Rim.

Tangguh was one of the main reasons for BP's takeover of the American oil company ARCO two years earlier; BP chief executive John Browne called the project a "crown jewel" in the shareholder meeting announcing the acquisition. The gas field was massive, with estimated reserves of 14.4 trillion cubic feet, enough to meet U.S. demand for natural gas for nearly eight months. The Tangguh project was a major prize in the increasingly fervent competition for natural resources, as oil and gas supplies in developed countries decline and companies have to go increasingly farther afield to meet global energy needs. While BP was buying its way into Indonesia and Russia, Chevron was doing the same into Burma and Ecuador with its acquisitions of Unocal and Texaco; Exxon merged with Mobil to expand its global reach; and Chinese extractive companies were beginning their forays into Africa.

The Tangguh project was technically straightforward: the gas field was large and close to the surface, making it easy to access, and BP had successfully built LNG plants all over the world. But never in a place like Papua.

A Sensitive Setting

Papua is one of the world's most remote spots, making up the western half of the island of New Guinea. (The eastern half is the independent nation of Papua New Guinea.) According to the 2000 census, Papua was home to approximately 2.1 million people spread out over an area about the size of California, which had nearly 34 million residents the same year. Much of the province is inaccessible, with few roads and varied and rough terrain that includes mangroves, rainforests, savanna, mountains, and even an equatorial glacier. New Guinea is a biodiversity hot spot, with 1 percent of the world's land mass but 5 percent of its plant and animal species. This was a place where one had to be careful where to step, for fear of crushing a unique moth or orchid, never mind where to put a new industrial facility.

With hundreds of tribal groups and languages, the region's mystique has been enhanced by occasional stories about a new tribe being "discovered"—as recently as 2010—and photos of highland tribesmen wearing little other than body paint and *kotekas*, dried gourds worn as sheaths over their penises.

Papua is closer to Australia than to its national capital, Jakarta, which is two thousand miles away. Whether Jakarta should be its capital at all is a point of contention for some. Papua belonged to the Netherlands until 1962, when Indonesian President Sukarno's threats to seize the province by force sent the province into temporary United Nations custody. In 1969 Jakarta conducted an "Act of Free Choice" referendum that included just over one thousand handpicked Papuans, who predictably voted to join Indonesia. A separatist movement remains alive today, with occasional violent clashes with the Indonesian military. Even the name of the province has been controversial: in the 1960s then-President Suharto named it "Irian Jaya," a name that locals never accepted but which retained some official legal status until 2007.

Some of the non-Papuan Indonesians I met seemed to view

Papua with disdain, as a backwater of primitive tribes. Papuans resemble Melanesians more than their fellow Indonesians, with dark skin, curly hair, and solid physiques, in contrast to their slighter, lighter-skinned Malay compatriots. Many Papuans are animist or Christian (the latter a legacy of Western missionaries), further setting them apart from Indonesia's Muslim majority. The capital's physical, psychological, and political distance from Papua results in a severe dearth of public services in the province, which ranks among the worst in the country for poverty, literacy, and life expectancy.

But Jakarta saw the rich natural resources in Papua that could fill its coffers. Like in many countries, in Indonesia oil and gas are owned by the national government, which hires companies like BP to develop those resources. The government and company typically sign a production sharing agreement, which means that the company invests the money to develop a project then has first claim to the revenues until it has recovered its costs, after which the profits are split between the company and the government.

Ideally, the national government would send some of its earnings back out to the people that had to put up with the companies in their backyards. But in countries without a long history of transparency and rule of law, the ruling elite uses the income to line its pockets rather than help its fellow citizens. As a result, the people living closest to the resource fail to benefit from its development, and ironically and tragically end up worse off. Communities in countries from Azerbaijan to Zimbabwe have suffered this phenomenon, known as the "resource curse" or the "paradox of plenty." People celebrate the discovery of oil, gas, or minerals, expecting jobs and wealth but getting nothing but environmental and social destruction.

All too often companies make these situations worse: by not

talking to their neighbor communities, wrongly assuming that the company's relationship with the national government is the only one that matters, and by paying bribes and hiring thuggish security guards to keep local people away.

Indonesia has more than its fair share of resource curse case studies after decades of President Suharto cutting deals with companies to enrich his family and cronies. The country's most notorious example was also in Papua, a few hundred miles from Tangguh: Freeport-McMoran's Grasberg copper and gold mine, one of the world's largest, has seen decades of violence. People who live near the mine hate the company for shutting them out of all but a few of the lowest-paying jobs, and for letting refuse from the mine flow for miles. The first time I flew over the Grasberg area on my way to Tangguh, I saw the vast gray wasteland and thought for a moment that it had snowed.

At the other end of the country, ExxonMobil's LNG plant in Aceh had to halt production for five months in 2001 because of the civil war going on around it. Some believe the company exacerbated the conflict: that year, eleven Acehnese filed suit against the company in U.S. federal court alleging that it provided buildings and supplies for Indonesian special forces "which were used by Indonesian 'Kopassus' (special forces) units to interrogate, torture and murder Achenese civilians suspected of engaging in separatist activities." As of 2013, the case had yet to be settled or adjudicated.

In 1999 Indonesia passed a law meant to address the concerns of its resource-rich provinces, namely Papua and Aceh, by sending a greater share of revenue back to regional governments. But the implementing regulations would take years to write, and Jakarta's efforts to split Papua into multiple provinces in the meantime were seen as attempts to divide and conquer. Even if the regulations were in place, it was likely that funds would have been siphoned off on their way out to the provinces: in 2001 and 2002, Transparency International's Corruption Perception Index rated Indonesia 1.9 out of 10, where 0 is "highly corrupt" and 10 is "very clean." Given the usual trajectory of extractive projects and the legacy of such developments in Indonesia in particular, it was easy to envision Tangguh going down the same path. But BP's chief executive at the time, John Browne, wanted to approach the project differently.

A Different Brand of Oilman

John Browne looked like the antithesis of the stereotypical oilman: a slight, soft-spoken opera lover whose attention to detail showed as much in his Savile Row suits and fine art collection as in his hands-on management of the company. Browne joined BP as a university apprentice in 1966 and rose through the exploration and production division to increasingly senior corporate positions until he was named chief executive in 1995. He then took BP from a two-pipeline company, with operations in Alaska and the North Sea of the United Kingdom, to a global superpower, buying up Amoco, ARCO, and Castrol.

Browne made BP a force to be reckoned with in economic terms, but also had a broader vision of the impact the company could have in the world. In 1996, he pulled BP out of the Global Climate Coalition, a lobbying group created to promote skepticism about climate change. In 1997 in a speech at Stanford University, Browne announced that there is now an "an effective consensus among the world's leading scientists and serious and well-informed people outside the scientific community that there is a discernible human influence on the climate," and that "it would be unwise and potentially dangerous to ignore the mounting concern." In 1998, in the speech I attended at Yale, Browne committed BP to cutting emissions 10 percent below 1990 levels by 2010—a target the company then met eight years ahead of schedule. In 2000, BP launched a new logo: a green, yellow, and white sunburst called Helios, after the Greek god of the sun, to "suggest heat, light, and nature." The logo was accompanied by a new slogan, "Beyond Petroleum."

These moves won Browne respect beyond his industry, with fellow British executives voting him "Most Admired Leader" four years in a row. He was knighted in 1998 and made a life peer in 2001. In 2002, the *Financial Times* ran a flattering profile anointing Browne "The Sun King."

Browne's legacy would be severely undermined a few years later by a number of operational disasters. But at the time, I saw the Browne that the public saw: someone fashioning himself as a different kind of oilman and BP as a different kind of oil company.

The son of an Auschwitz survivor, Browne frequently spoke about the company's social as well as environmental role. At a conference in 1998, he said that business is "not victory or conquest, but a long-term commitment to the people you work with, the people with whom you do business and the society of which we are all part."

Browne was not just speaking theoretically. In the 1980s BP began to explore in Colombia, and by 1991 confirmed substantial reserves in a remote part of Casanare province in the eastern part of the country. Colombia was BP's first foray outside of the U.K. and North America since the nationalization of oil production across the Middle East in the 1970s. In unfamiliar territory, BP did not get off to a good start. Migrants flowed into the area seeking either employment or illicit ways of capitalizing on the company's entry, and guerilla groups followed. BP facilities were sabotaged and contractors kidnapped. Seeing no choice but to pay for protection, BP consequently was seen not as victim but as accomplice in the assassination of a community leader and violence by mercenaries. The accusations of complicity were repeated in numerous television programs, the U.K. House of Commons, and the European Parliament.

Multiple investigations found no evidence to support the allegations, but it was clear that there was a deep mistrust of BP in the communities of Casanare. BP had failed to secure what has become commonly known as the "social license to operate": permission from not just government regulators but stakeholders affected by the company's operations. BP then worked hard to engage with communities and establish programs ranging from human rights training for the military to local procurement to a popular *Time for Peace* radio show promoting tolerance and violence prevention. Conditions and relationships improved dramatically, but BP had learned its lesson.

The Tangguh project in Papua was an opportunity for Browne to show that the company's problems in Colombia were aberrations. As Browne later wrote in his autobiography, "Leaders are not perfect; they are bound to make mistakes as they do new things. But they must never make the same mistake twice."

The resettlement of Tanah Merah presented the first most obvious challenge for Tangguh. People all over the world are forced to move by their governments to make way for large projects deemed to be in the public interest, such as dams, highways, power plants, or subways. Many countries require consultation and compensation for the people forced to relocate. However, a 1960 Indonesian law stated that land rights cannot be in conflict with national interests, which gave the central government the right to seize land. There was little documentation of any consultation with the people of Tanah Merah, just a 1999 agreement in which ARCO agreed to pay the communities fifteen to thirty Indonesian rupiah (a fraction of a penny) per square meter for their land, a price that the villagers now considered unfair. There were no analogous situations in Papua to provide a benchmark for land values; the central government had given Freeport the land for its mine without compensating the local population, which was part of why company–community relations were so bad there. The national government expressed no concerns with the ARCO arrangement and were eager for BP to build the plant and get the revenues flowing in. But they wouldn't have to live with angry communities on their doorstep.

A New Frontier

When I moved to Indonesia in August 2000, human rights and the resource curse were not supposed to be my focus. I had spent the previous summer as an MBA intern in BP's London headquarters, primarily working with John Browne's chief policy advisor. I enjoyed studying and discussing geopolitical issues with him, but when I joined the company full-time I felt obligated to apply my new MBA skills crunching data as a commercial analyst—my notion of what a real businessperson did. I joined BP Indonesia's commercial team, which was in the midst of gathering historical financial and production figures for the ARCO assets that BP had acquired. My job was to use that data to help analyze how these projects fit into BP's regional and global portfolio.

I was looking forward to my new role, but given my interest in the role of business in society I had also chatted with the head of the small government and public affairs team for Tangguh, and we agreed to check in from time to time about whether there might be an opportunity for me to help out. I took advantage of my seat near that team, blatantly eavesdropping on their conversations and asking about their work. Their world of resettlement and human rights was turning out to be much more intriguing to me than barrels per day and return on capital employed.

The opportunity to get more involved with their world soon presented itself. John Browne instituted peer reviews in BP, where anyone stuck on a problem could bring together specialists from other comparable projects. Usually peer reviews were on technical issues like gas flaring or water management, but the Indonesia staff wanted to try a social peer review for Tangguh and asked if I would like to organize it. I jumped at the chance.

I spent a few months coordinating travel logistics, setting up meetings and sorting out the agenda, while still doing my commercial job. The roster for the peer review included two BP executives from Australia who had worked with indigenous communities; BP's vice president for health, safety, and environment policies and practices; a member of BP's Global Social Investment team; and two external experts, an anthropologist who had spent years in Papua and an environmental consultant.

After a daylong briefing in our Jakarta offices and an early dinner, we headed to the airport for our evening flight. Nineteen hundred miles and two time zones later, we landed just before sunrise on Biak Island, just northwest of Papua's mainland. In the one-room airport, men piled luggage from our flight in one corner while others lined the walls smoking cigarettes. One came up and showed us his BP identification card—as the only crowd of Westerners, we weren't difficult to spot—and we walked out to his van.

After a nap, shower, and powdered eggs and toast at a basic local hotel, where the only other guests were a few Chinese businessmen, we were taken back to the airport for an hour-long flight on an eighteen-seat turboprop plane deeper into the province. The landscape varied from dense rainforest to clear-cut open land, pockmarked by bomb craters left by Japanese warplanes dropping off unused munitions during World War II. We landed at an airstrip where we watched a BP safety video then boarded a helicopter for the forty-five-minute trip to Bintuni Bay.

I'd never been in a helicopter before, and leaned as close to the window as my seatbelt would allow. I saw no people, just occasional flocks of birds bursting from the trees. As we approached the bay I spotted our landing pad, a brown square with a white "H," and on the horizon an exploration rig.

I had seen sketches of what the plant would look like, a modern complex of gleaming silver buildings, circled by trucks and cars filled with men in hardhats. I tried to visualize the images from those sketches on the scene below me, mentally replacing swathes of forest with steel and concrete. Suddenly the ride got uncomfortable: the cabin felt tiny and the chopper noise was deafening. I mopped my brow, tugged at my lifejacket and took a swig of water, and realized where my discomfort was coming from. For the first time, I was seeing what BP was in the business of doing, and it was literally making me sick.

I turned to Kathryn Shanks, BP's health, safety, and environment vice president, who saw the distress on my face. "That's why we're here," she said. "We're going to get this right. Who else would bring all of this high-paid help here to do this?" I suspected she was right, but still had an uneasy feeling in my stomach.

We touched down on the landing pad, where three Papuans were lined up in a tight row holding one fire hose and wearing boxy black rubber fire suits, yellow hard hats, and dark visors, looking like Lego men. Our Indonesian colleague Erwin Maryoto told us those were new hires from the nearby villages, being trained for jobs at our base camp.

Erwin had joined ARCO as a geoscientist and been part of the team conducting the first seismic surveys of the area in the mid-1990s. A natural extrovert, he always ended up being the ARCO staffer to communicate to local residents what the company was doing. When ARCO realized that someone needed to work on community affairs full-time, Erwin was the natural choice. By the time BP took over ARCO, Erwin had earned the trust and respect of local residents and proved a valuable interlocutor between them and the company.

The camp manager walked us to the barracks to drop off our bags, then we all headed out on foot to tour the area. In the first village, we were greeted by three men and four women in grass skirts, decorated with white body paint; one of the men had a small drum, another a gong. They shuffled and chanted in unison, then parted to make way for a group of eight younger girls in grass skirts and royal blue tube tops who had different moves and a higher-pitched chant. The rest of the village stood around and watched in SpongeBob T-shirts and European soccer jerseys. This scene repeated itself in the other villages we visited around the bay.

At the first two welcome ceremonies I was in awe, thrilled to be witnessing what I knew few others would ever see. But my excitement gave way to embarrassment as I noticed their stoic expressions. Were they simply the expressions of people conducting rituals for real, not for show? Or were they bored, or resentful for having to take time out to welcome these invaders? Erwin assured me that the villagers would have considered it inappropriate and disrespectful to let us in without the ritual.

I believed him, but still felt like a guest who had already over-stayed her welcome but was about to move in anyway.

First Look

I'm not the only Corporate Idealist who had an adverse reaction to seeing my company's impacts for the first time. Darrell Doren, global compliance director for the labeling and packaging company Avery Dennison, told me that he got his dream job in 2003, working with Ford in China to buy manufactured parts for export. On his second day at work, he walked into a potential supplier factory for the first time and was shocked at conditions that he described as "Dickensian": soot-covered walls, people "hoping as much as I was that they went home safe at the end of the day."

Darrell was appalled. "I can't be the guy that encourages this type of activity," he thought at the time. "I sat down with my boss the next day—this is Wednesday after coming to China. And I said, 'You know what? I cannot participate in a system that allows this to happen.'

"He said, 'It sounds like you just volunteered to run our social compliance program.' I said, 'What does that mean?' He said, 'Our CEO has said that we can source as much as we want to in China as long as we do it responsibly. We don't know what that means, so we set up a team to start figuring it out. It sounds like you're the guy.'" Darrell stayed at Ford for five more years in supply chain sustainability, then moved to Avery Dennison in 2008.

Similarly, my first visit to Tangguh was at times uncomfortable but ended up shaping my career. After the peer review trip, I was daunted by the challenges that our visitors identified but inspired by seeing Tangguh firsthand and by the commitment of my colleagues to address what we euphemistically called "nontechnical" or "above ground" risks. When I left business school I shared the assumption with many of my classmates that we would do time in the private sector to bank some skills and savings and eventually go back to a role that was explicitly about making the world a better place, presumably in an NGO or government agency. But in Indonesia with BP, I had already stumbled into a role that was about helping people and communities.

Of course, mine wasn't a purely altruistic endeavor. I was to help people and communities whose lives would be upended by BP's entry, in part to prevent unrest that could jeopardize BP's business. But my belief—which I felt my BP bosses shared—was that my goal was to align the interests of the company and the community, not to compensate for or distract from wrongdoing.

I wanted to focus on community issues full-time. But I still felt some obligation to use the spreadsheet skills I'd learned, both for what I understood to be the path to success in business and to prove to myself that getting an MBA wasn't a waste of time and money. I never would have found myself working for BP had I not gone to business school, but I still felt conflicted about not flexing my new quantitative muscles.

I had felt a kindred spirit in Kathryn Shanks, the environmental vice president on the Tangguh trip who had found a home at BP. I wrote her an e-mail:

It was such a pleasure to spend time with you. The week was a powerful one for me; I'm considering a head-first full-time dive into the community development aspects of Tangguh, trying to quit worrying about my sense of obligation to work on my commercial skills. My thinking could change on this, but it seems as though this is such a unique time, with the opportunities and challenges that we face here, and that the team here has a need that I could meet. And if I am excellent in this arena (where it might be easier for me to distinguish myself, as opposed to the commercial field), I will still have all doors open for me for whatever I want to do next. Do you think this makes sense?

She wrote back two days later:

I think that you could pursue the social agenda to your benefit and perhaps even weave in some commercial thinking—esp about creating a sustainable economy and profitable community based conservation for the Tangguh area. It is probably cutting edge stuff that would continue to open quite a few doors for you. You may even create a new discipline within BP!

We had no idea how right she would turn out to be. At the time, this "new discipline" was just starting to take shape; a few companies were setting up corporate social responsibility programs, but I didn't yet know anyone who had made a career out of managing human rights for a company. At Tangguh and in my own career, there was little precedent to follow.

No Road Map

Corporate Idealists often have to operate without a road map. Doug Cahn told me about conducting Reebok's first factory audit in the early 1990s, before such audits were commonplace. He had joined the company in 1991 to manage Reebok's program honoring human rights defenders, an outgrowth of its sponsorship of an Amnesty International concert tour. Not long after he joined he suggested to his boss that, given the work they were doing to acknowledge human rights work around the world, they should probably take a look at human rights conditions in their own supply chain. At the time, sweatshops weren't yet in the public conscience. It would be another five years before television host Kathie Lee Gifford would cry on air after hearing that her clothing line was made in Honduran sweatshops and seven years before Phil Knight would admit that his company, Nike, had "become synonymous with slave wages, forced overtime and arbitrary abuse."

Doug's bosses at Reebok agreed that they should examine their supply chain, so he took the long journey with Reebok's head of internal audit from Boston to Jakarta, where they met up with the general manager for manufacturing, who was based in Hong Kong. They drove to Tangerang, an industrial area outside the capital, were greeted warmly by the factory manager, ushered into a conference room, served tea, and left to collect their thoughts. "The three of us sat down in the conference room and we looked at each other and said, 'Well, now what do we do?'" Armed with clipboards, notes on international labor conventions, and Polaroid cameras, they fanned out across the factory. "For each incident where we thought this may be a problem, the three of us had to regroup and test each other's sensibility. 'Did *you* think that was a problem? Did *you* think that was a problem?' We did that a lot in order to come to a consensus of what good behavior was. There were no benchmarks, really." From there, Doug established a factory monitoring program at Reebok that has been considered best-in-class, and became one of the world's leading experts in supply chain labor standards.

Similarly, we didn't yet have a clear plan for Tangguh, but it was clear that there was a lot to do. The peer review team felt strongly that the resettlement presented a major potential risk to Tangguh's success and to BP's global reputation. The issue escalated back to London, where John Browne himself expressed discomfort at causing people to relocate. The Tangguh team was directed to consider alternate locations for the plant.

The engineers went back to the drawing board, the government affairs and commercial teams discussed the implications of changing our plans, and a few weeks later we all met and studied the options. We considered building a floating facility, but there was too much uncertainty about technical feasibility and safety. There was only one other onshore site where the ground might have been solid enough to support the plant, but the land was sloping, swampy, and too far from the part of the bay deep enough to accommodate LNG tankers. We also estimated a two-year wait to acquire the additional land rights, which we thought would be unacceptable to the Indonesian government, customers, and BP's partners in the project. So back to Tanah Merah it was, but I was impressed with the rigor of the exercise we had gone through.

Browne accepted the necessity of the resettlement, but instructed us to start the consultation process over and make sure it was done to the highest international standards, bringing in whatever expert advice we needed to get it right.

Resettlement

For resettlement, the authoritative standards were written by the World Bank, specifically by Michael Cernea, a gray-bearded Romanian-born sociologist. During our first phone conversation, Cernea listened intently to my description of the project until I told him the number of households that had to move. "127?!" He had just returned from India advising on a project that caused the displacement of forty thousand people. Getting the resettlement right is critical to Tangguh's success no matter how few people were affected, I said. There were solid business reasons for wanting to ensure that our neighbors were satisfied. But even if there weren't, who would want to be part of destroying a community? Browne had set out an ambitious goal: make Tangguh a good thing for the people of Papua—essentially, refute the resource curse. Intrigued by the challenge and never having worked directly with a company, Cernea agreed to advise us.

Cernea hosted a workshop in D.C. to explain to Tangguh's executives what a proper resettlement process would entail, and we worked out a detailed action plan. Cernea later admitted to me that he was initially concerned about BP using him as a "fig leaf" for public relations purposes. But his skepticism faded as we adopted his recommendations that cost the project time and money, including assigning senior engineers to oversee the resettlement full-time.

I headed back out to Papua for a community meeting to announce that we would be starting the consultation process over. By that point I could carry on a basic conversation in Indonesian, but only a few of the villagers spoke the national language and the local languages were completely different. I didn't understand most of the exchange that ensued, but it didn't take a professional interpreter to know that the villagers weren't happy.

"They want to move now," my colleague Erwin explained to me. "ARCO told them they were going to move three years ago, so they haven't done any maintenance on their houses or plots of land." I thought the village looked a little shabby, but I didn't have any reference point for what it should look like.

"But we want to do this to international standards," we insisted to the assembled group. "We're trying to protect your rights."

Again, it didn't take a U.N. translator for me to get the gist of their response, which was that they were not impressed with our efforts to "protect" them. I'd learned from my research and from Cernea that a well-documented consultation process helps resolve the disputes that inevitably arise years or even generations later. But the people of Tanah Merah wanted to proceed with their move—even to a site that we thought was far from ideal—and we wanted to delay that. Who did these foreigners think they were, claiming to know what was in their best interests?

Over the subsequent weeks we negotiated a timeline, explaining each step in the resettlement process and why it was important, and working to understand the community's priorities and concerns. On Cernea's advice we built a model house in the village, with local residents taking part in the design and construction. The community seemed happy with the house, until one of them came to our base camp and said they wanted brick houses. Brick retains heat—unsuitable for Papua's tropical climate—and is not local to the area, unlike the wood used in the model. We want brick, they declared.

If this was a truly consultative process, we had to listen to what they wanted, but what if they were clearly making a bad choice? Through further consultation, it came out that one Tanah Merah resident had spent time in the nearby city of Sorong and came back believing that brick was a sign of progress and convinced others of the same. Thankfully, after three more months of consultations and conversations about the availability and suitability of brick, an all-village meeting resulted in a majority vote in favor of wood.

Security and Human Rights

If the resettlement seemed daunting, it was only because I didn't yet understand what it would mean to work with the Indonesian military. The reputation of the armed forces was embodied in the commander assigned to our area: Major General Mahidin Simbolon, named by the Indonesia–Timor Leste Commission for Truth and Friendship as having contributed to gross human rights violations around the 1999 referendum that led to East Timor's independence from Indonesia.

Echoes of BP in Colombia and of the Ken Saro-Wiwa case loomed large. Saro-Wiwa was a Nigerian writer and activist who helped found the Movement for the Survival of the Ogoni People, mobilizing thousands to protest pollution by Shell's operations in the Niger Delta. In 1995, Saro-Wiwa and eight of his colleagues were tried and convicted of murder and hanged. Saro-Wiwa's supporters pleaded with Shell to use its leverage with the Nigerian government to call off the execution. At the time Shell demurred, saying, "It is not for commercial organizations like Shell to interfere in the legal process of a sovereign state such as Nigeria," although since then the company has said it made appeals that were ignored.

A 1965 presidential decree spelled out the Indonesian military's duty to protect vital national assets, which Tangguh was. The military was stripped of that duty in 2005. But five years earlier we couldn't very well demand that the military stay out of the area or swap out the commander. Accepting the status quo clearly had its own risks, however, such as whether

BP might be complicit in any human rights abuses that security forces committed. We might supply them with equipment that could be used for nefarious purposes, as ExxonMobil was alleged to have done in Aceh, or signal that our desire for a safe operating environment was to be achieved by any means necessary—which could be interpreted as license to kill.

There was one set of new international guidelines that we could follow: the Voluntary Principles on Security and Human Rights, a code of conduct that arose from BP's troubles in Colombia and Shell's in Nigeria, developed by those two companies and others in collaboration with Human Rights Watch and other human rights groups and the U.S. and U.K. governments. With guidance on risk assessment and on working with public and private security providers, the Voluntary Principles would be useful, but we needed more help.

We decided to do what every complex organization with big challenges and some money does: commission a study. Speaking with colleagues in London and human rights experts, we came up with the idea of commissioning a human rights impact assessment. Projects with big physical footprints routinely conduct environmental impact assessments, some of which include social issues, but those tend to be focused on direct impacts such as how the air and water quality will change and how many people will be employed directly by the project. We were doing one of those studies for Tangguh as required by the government, but it wasn't touching upon the more complex issues that we were concerned about: How could we ensure that the military could play its legally-mandated role, but that the rights of local people would be protected? How could we abide by international human rights standards, for example on the right to self-determination or the right not to be deprived of property, when Indonesian law was silent and in some places contradicting such standards? We didn't have any examples to follow—to our knowledge, no such study had ever been done for a company.

We fleshed out the idea with human rights experts and hired Gare Smith and Bennett Freeman to do the impact assessment. Both of them had worked in multinational companies and the U.S. State Department. Gare also served as vice chairman of the board of the International Campaign for Tibet, and his law firm, Foley Hoag, was the first in the world to have a corporate social responsibility practice. While at the State Department Bennett spearheaded the development of the Voluntary Principles on Security and Human Rights, the guidance on security provision for extractive companies that was very relevant to Tangguh.

I knew Gare and Bennett to be extroverted and friendly, and thought they would be capable of both interacting with the wide range of people who had something to say about Tangguh and presenting advice in such a way that BP executives would listen.

Gare and Bennett interviewed experts and government officials in D.C. and London while I planned meetings for them in Indonesia for October 2001.

On the night of September 11th in Jakarta—morning in New York—I was on a girls' night out with women I had met during the year I'd been there. We had met at a bar for cocktails and were about to move on to dinner when three of our phones rang at once. "That's weird," we said, fumbling through our purses. "A plane hit the World Trade Center," someone said. "A small plane?" "No, a 747!" Without saying goodbye we scattered into cars and taxis, cell phones pressed to our ears.

I spent the next three days alone in my apartment, watching the towers in my hometown collapse over and over on television, trying in vain to call friends in Manhattan, told by BP to stay home until further notice. We postponed Gare and Bennett's trip. I called my contacts in Papua to tell them we would reschedule their meetings. They kindly asked whether my family was all right, and expressed some wonder at how events halfway around the world could affect life in Papua. I didn't have a good response, but tried the common practice of Indonesian-izing an English word by replacing "-tion" with "-asi." "*Globalisasi?*" I shrugged.

Avoiding Complicity

In the subsequent months, relations between Papuans and the military worsened. On November 10, 2001, Theys Eluay, the sixty-four-year-old leader of the Papuan Presidium Council and one of the leading voices for Papuan independence, was found dead in his car, asphyxiated. He had just attended a ceremony at the local headquarters of Kopassus, the Indonesian army's special forces.

Our civil society and human rights contacts in Papua, Jakarta, and even London and Washington started asking what we were going to do. What, about a murder that had nothing to do with the company, the investigation of which was being conducted by a sovereign government? BP is one of the biggest players in Papua, they said, and therefore has a responsibility to speak out against such an egregious mockery of justice— particularly one committed by the same entity BP would be contracting with.

We were tempted to condemn the murder, but were mindful of antagonizing our host government. BP had gotten into trouble not long before for trying to take a principled stance in a difficult place. In 1999, the NGO Global Witness (best known for bringing the issue of blood diamonds to the world's attention) published a report called *A Crude Awakening,* condemning corruption in Angola and urging oil companies operating there, including BP, to declare all payments to the government and push for greater transparency and accountability.

According to David Rice, BP's policy director at the time, the company realized that the conditions Global Witness described could threaten whether local people saw benefits from the oil, leading to local and international anger that could put BP's operations at risk. "We thought if we don't do something about this, it will become Nigeria, and look what Nigeria did for Shell," David told me. "It wasn't, 'Aren't we wonderfully moral people,' but 'This is a big business risk, a real operational risk.' I personally thought it was a moral issue, but there was also a strong business case for taking action."

John Browne felt the same way; he later wrote in his autobiography that publishing payments could pressure government "to use the money in ways that would benefit a broader population. And it might help us by improving political and economic stability in the country."

BP determined it could publish payments in the United Kingdom in its required filings there. Global Witness put out a press release calling BP's decision "an excellent move." But the announcement provoked a stern letter from the head of Sonangol, the Angolan state oil company, asserting that publication would violate confidentiality clauses in BP's contract and constitute grounds for expropriation. But BP did indeed publish payment data in the U.K., and has not only continued to operate in Angola but become one of its largest foreign investors.

In Indonesia, a few staff and advisors suggested that we place a condolence message about Theys Eluay in a local newspaper, assuring us that such gestures by companies were commonplace. On November 21, 2001, the following appeared in Indonesian in the *Cendrawasih Post*, Papua's main daily:

> BP and Pertamina [the state oil and gas agency]
> Conveying Sorrowful Condolence over the Death of
> Mister THEYS HIYO ELUAY
> on 11 November 2001
> in Jayapura, Papua
> May his honored soul be received by God
> And may his bereaved family attain
> Resolve and strength through faith to face this
>   misfortune.

To my knowledge, we never heard any reactions to the message.

By the time Gare Smith and Bennett Freeman arrived in Indonesia in January 2002 the murder investigation had made no progress, and it topped the agenda of many of the people they met with. Their schedule included a meeting with none other than the infamous General Simbolon. We decided it would be best if BP staff joined them for this one; we had stayed out of most of their meetings so everyone could speak freely about the company, although we weren't sure whether anyone really made a distinction between BP's employees and our slew of consultants. With a meeting this sensitive, we didn't want any chance of mixed messages.

Rich Herold, a senior government relations official and Asia expert in BP's Washington D.C. office, flew out to join us for the Simbolon meeting. Our Indonesian colleagues thought it best if they did not attend, believing that any mention of the Eluay murder should come from foreigners, who might be forgiven some ignorance in raising such an impolitic topic. (Some of them also expressed disbelief that we were voluntarily sitting down with a man alleged to have been involved in war crimes.)

The sun beat down on our jeeps as we were driven to the military command post in Jayapura, the provincial capital. A soldier waved us into a meeting hall, empty except for a few folding chairs and a sunglasses-clad Simbolon, a lieutenant, and a man in civilian clothes. As we shook their hands, General Simbolon said a few words in Indonesian, after which the civilian translator said, "The general apologizes that his English is not very good, but welcomes you to his post."

We exchanged pleasantries about BP's plans to develop Tangguh and hopefully bring development and peace to the people of Papua, all awkwardly communicated by the translator. Then Rich took a deep breath.

"General Simbolon, we have to tell you that the murder of Theys Eluay is causing great concern, not just in Indonesia but in London, where our chief executive sits, and Washington, D.C., where I come from. Our investors, our congressmen, and the media are asking about the case, and wondering whether BP can operate in an environment where such a crime might go unpunished. BP is committed to maintaining its investment in Papua, but we needed to convey to you the hope from the international community that Mr. Eluay's killers will be brought to justice."

The translator's jaw dropped. He stared at Rich for a moment, then started to speak, but the general slowly raised his hand, stopping the translator mid-breath. After a long pause, he spoke, in perfect English.

"This will be like your JFK assassination: no one will ever know who did it."

We were speechless. The general stood up and the other two hopped up alongside him. "Thank you for visiting today," he said. "I wish you and Tangguh the best of luck."

I was glad that we voiced our concerns, but I suspected the general wasn't going to rush to discipline his colleagues. Why should he listen to us? BP had no influence over the military. Indonesian President Megawati Sukarnoputri might respond if we threatened to withdraw from the project or even the country if the situation didn't improve; but even she wasn't seen as having much control over the armed forces. Plus, a threat from BP to withdraw from the country wouldn't be credible: we had invested far too much money to walk away. Technology or pharmaceutical companies can move research teams and manufacturers can source from different factories, but oil and mining companies are stuck where the resources are—and typically invest hundreds of millions of dollars or more before seeing a dime of revenue.

Had Eluay lived in one of the villages around the Tangguh project and been explicitly protesting the company's presence, echoes of the Saro-Wiwa case might have been louder. No one ever suggested that BP was complicit in the Eluay murder. Nonetheless, it was clear that enough people viewed BP as so influential that we had an obligation to speak.

But we couldn't exactly put out a press release saying that we had brought up the matter with the man directly. It wasn't hard to imagine retaliation if we issued a public rebuke, whether direct threats to our staff or assets or more insidious undermining of Papua's stability as the military had done around Freeport's mine. We would probably continue to field accusations that we had remained silent, and couldn't give any proof to deny them. In 2003, seven members of the army's special forces received twenty-four- to forty-two-month jail sentences for

Eluay's murder, an outcome criticized by human rights activists for the brevity of the sentences and the low rank of those convicted.

One of the frustrations of the Corporate Idealist is not being able to talk about what his or her company is doing, especially when it is exactly what the public would want. In 2013, a handful of tech companies were caught up in revelations about secret U.S. intelligence-gathering programs. Anger at the government for conducting such extensive surveillance spread to the companies that were compelled by law to assist. Some of the companies privately fought government requests and lobbied for greater transparency. But under the U.S. Patriot Act and the Foreign Intelligence Surveillance Act, the companies could not acknowledge the existence of government demands, never mind any challenges or lobbying that they engaged in—even after news of the surveillance programs leaked.

Some ten years after our meeting with General Simbolon, I asked Rich Herold (who has since left BP) for his reflections. He came to believe that our principled approach was naïve, a tick-box exercise to satisfy ourselves and anyone we could have told privately but not making "one iota" of difference to the situation on the ground.

Gare disagreed. "Who knows?" he told me when I shared Rich's opinion. "Expressing concern may have prevented the murder of other activists who were next in line to be eliminated."

Mila Rosenthal, a longtime human rights activist who led Amnesty International USA's work on business from 2003 to 2007, agrees that speaking up was right:

> There are risky business choices. But some companies had spoken out in difficult places and were on the record as having done so, so it did suggest that there was

more that companies could do that was safer than they thought it would be. My perspective as an advocate is, it's almost always better to bring it up, it's always better to say that there are lines you can't cross, it's always better to say something is wrong. I understand that whether or not a company should say publicly that they raised a concern is a separate question. But I do think companies should speak out more.

While the definition of corporate complicity in human rights abuses continues to evolve, the United Nations Global Compact's seven thousand–plus company signatories have committed to a set of principles that includes the following: "Businesses should make sure they are not complicit in human rights abuses." The compact explains that complicity includes an act or omission by a company "that 'helps' (facilitates, legitimizes, assists, encourages, etc.) another, in some way, to carry out a human rights abuse." Failure to condemn abuses could amount to encouragement, which BP certainly wanted to avoid.

Assessment and Disclosure

Gare and Bennett submitted the Tangguh Human Rights Impact Assessment in April 2002. It included useful recommendations for our relationship with the military: that we should establish clear rules for providing them with equipment; adhere to international standards like the Voluntary Principles on Security and Human Rights; develop programs with organizations like the International Committee of the Red Cross to train soldiers in appropriate use of force; and work with the military to set up their command post near enough that they could respond in case of emergency, but far enough that they weren't causing tension in the communities near the plant.

The assessment also helpfully explained how human rights expectations differ from what the company was required to do by the Indonesian government. Human rights as spelled out in international agreements may or may not be reflected in local and national law, but comprise a set of standards to which multinational companies can be held to account by campaigners, investors, and other stakeholders. The assessment framed the issues in such a way that we weren't just making sure people were safe and able to voice their views, we were respecting their right to life and freedom of opinion and expression. This seemed on the surface like a semantic exercise, but those semantics meant a shift in perspective: we were no longer taking a purely company-centric view of Tangguh, but were recognizing that our neighbors had rights that were, in the words of the Universal Declaration of Human Rights, "equal and inalienable." As Chris Avery, founder of the Business and Human Rights Resource Centre, has written:

> A CSR approach tends to be top-down: a company decides what issues it wishes to address. Perhaps contributing to community education, healthcare or the arts. Or donating to disaster relief abroad. Or taking steps to encourage staff diversity or reduce pollution. These voluntary initiatives should be welcomed. But a human rights approach is different. It is not top-down, but bottom-up—with the individual at the centre, not the corporation.

The report led to us developing a community-based security program, not unlike the community policing programs that some U.S. cities have found effective, giving residents ownership over the safety of their neighborhoods. We hired local people as security guards, giving them batons but no guns, and brought in human rights trainers for them. We worked with the military to establish its main base in the nearby town of Babo, which was a few miles away and had some shops and infrastructure.

I was eager to share the report with the many people who Gare and Bennett had interviewed, from local residents to Indonesian academics to international development and security experts, and the wider world. I spoke with our communications department about putting it on bp.com and translating it into Indonesian. They seemed enthusiastic and said they just had to run it by our lawyers, as they did any public announcement.

Back at my desk, I got a call from the legal department. "You want to publish this human rights report?"

"Yes, of course, that was one of the main reasons for doing it."

"But it says bad things about the Indonesian military."

Was it news that General Simbolon had been accused of human rights abuses? "But everything they wrote about them is already in the public domain!" I doubted General Simbolon would ever read the report, but having met the man in person and knowing his history, I could hardly challenge the widespread fear of him and the organization he controlled.

Our lawyers were concerned about the report's assertion of bad behavior by a number of parties, from the military to other companies in the area. Even though the report was not written by the company, they wanted assurance that there was ample evidence to back up these statements so we wouldn't be sued for libel, and that we understood that we would likely antagonize the people and organizations named.

They also expressed a concern that would become a

recurring theme in the subsequent years that I continued to work on human rights with companies, not just with BP: whether the report itself was providing evidence that we knew about serious risks around Tangguh but proceeded with the project anyway. Lawyers fretted that this could increase potential liability should these worst-case scenarios come to pass.

This seemed to me like a ludicrous argument. If we took it upon ourselves to investigate the risks, wouldn't that reflect favorably on us? If we didn't act upon what we found, that could indicate negligence; but surely acting upon the findings was the purpose of the exercise, and if we failed to do so we should indeed be found negligent? Gare continues to encounter this attitude in his legal practice today, and cannot believe that some companies take what he described as an ostrich's head-in-the-sand approach: "How is that good for your business?" he said to me. "If you don't assess your risks, how can you possibly be responsible to your shareholders?"

We had already assessed our risks in commissioning the study, but publishing it in full was beyond what we could convince our lawyers to do. We published the two and a half pages of bullet points summarizing Gare and Bennett's recommendations and a one-page conclusion, along with a company response. The full sixty-page version of the human rights impact assessment taunted me from my shelf. I considered leaking it to one of my journalist friends, but thought that would lack integrity and be a career-limiting move. I was disappointed that the full discussion of Tangguh's context and challenges wouldn't be seen beyond BP's proverbial walls, but consoled myself with the fact that I had survived my first battle with corporate lawyers and come up with a workable compromise. A few NGOs were also disappointed by the lack of full disclosure, boycotting one of the public meetings where Gare and Bennett presented the summary.

Such compromises are a typical part of life for the Corporate Idealist. "We do make those kinds of trade-offs," Monica Gorman, head of corporate compliance of New Balance told me. "At the end of the day my question is, do I think I did the best I could? I can live with myself if I believe I did. It's not always the way you want it to play out." Many Corporate Idealists I spoke with talked about having to pick one's battles in service of being able to effect meaningful change over the long run.

Looking back on the report more than ten years later, Bennett told me that he still agrees that it should not have been published in full, that his and Gare's mandate "was to be absolutely unsparing in our analysis and prescriptions. The whole point of the report was to put forward the kinds of recommendations that if they 'fell off the truck' could cause a big problem. The innovation when it came to transparency and disclosure was in commissioning it, publicly saying so, then summarizing the recommendations and doing stakeholder engagement around them. This was already setting the bar at an unprecedented high level. It would be irresponsible to go further."

More importantly, Bennett said he views the report as a major milestone, not just for BP or even the extractive industry. It would become clear in subsequent years that the human rights impact assessment proved useful for Tangguh, but also turned out to be a model for business worldwide as other companies started seeing the need to assess their human rights risks and other stakeholders realized that such studies should be required, particularly in complex situations. For example, in 2009 Yahoo! purchased Maktoob, a web portal founded in Jordan. Yahoo! conducted a human rights impact assessment that resulted in recommendations to continue Maktoob's policy of not storing user data locally and to establish a terms of service under the jurisdiction that would provide the most stringent protections for user data and free expression. "Those were all decisions that the company might not have known to make," Ebele Okobi, head of Yahoo!'s Business and Human Rights Program told me, "had we not done a human rights impact assessment."

Buying Time

The BP executives who focused on the technical and commercial aspects of Tangguh—building the plant and selling the gas—understood how important it was that we build good relationships with the local community. Nonetheless, they occasionally expressed concern about the time it would take to conduct the consultation process we outlined, particularly since we couldn't specify a number of meetings or a schedule for when we would be finished; we were done when the community seemed to understand and support what we were doing. Such a vague, open-ended process was antithetical to the usual way of operating for a company driven by Gantt charts and budgets—"the tyranny of project schedules," as one colleague put it.

But getting local support was essential before there were any visible signs of construction, or else the villagers would think we were proceeding with our plans regardless of what we said. As we could see at Freeport's Grasberg mine and Exxon-Mobil's Arun field in Aceh, antagonizing communities was not just ill-advised but expensive: ExxonMobil's 2001 four-month shutdown of its Aceh plant because of the surrounding social unrest was reported to have cost the company anywhere from $100 million to $350 million. A *Forbes* article said that Freeport spent $28 million in 2010 on security at Grasberg, up from $22 million in 2009.

In August 2002, Tangguh lost a bid to sell its gas to a

terminal being built in Guangdong, China. An LNG field in Australia that had been operating for years (and was partly owned by BP) won the contract. The winning bid and evaluations were confidential, but one of the many rumors I heard was that Chinese government officials had considered more than price in deciding against Tangguh: they believed that the social and environmental risks in Papua were so great that they doubted Tangguh would be up and running when promised.

Not only had we won more time to conduct community consultations, but our case for doing so was strengthened.

The Big Picture

As BP learned in Colombia, big projects in remote places attract not just money but new residents, particularly where roads make migration easy. Thinking there might be jobs available, people move right up to the site and stay whether or not they can find work. Shantytowns pop up as people tap into the power grid, and those who can't find legitimate sources of income resort to crime and prostitution.

The area around Tangguh couldn't sustain much population growth, socially or environmentally. We worked with the government on an agreement not to build any roads into the site and to bring in construction materials by boat or air—costly, but deemed to be worth avoiding migration and all of the problems that would come with it. We had acquired land rights to about eleven square miles beyond the footprint of the plant to maintain as a green buffer zone.

We posted signs throughout the region and spread the word through our community liaison officers and other Papuan contacts that people would only be hired in the three cities in the province, not at the Tangguh site. The exception would be one construction job for each household in the nearby villages. We also stipulated that when workers finished their three-week shift, during which they would be staying in a closed camp, they had to return to those cities in order to get paid. Experience at other locations where the resource curse has taken hold has shown that if you hand people wages in the middle of nowhere when they are far from their families, opportunities to spend money suddenly appear in the form of brothels, bars, and gambling houses. Those entrepreneurial ventures are followed by seedy characters who smell extortion opportunities, then by police who come in ostensibly to keep order but want their cut as well. The police are then seen by the military as encroaching on its turf; a larger army presence soon follows.

It was clear that the myriad issues we had to deal with—security, resettlement, migration, fishing rights—were not only complex but interconnected, and none could be addressed in isolation. Thankfully, Browne was still giving us permission and funding to bring in all the expertise we needed, in part due to the steady drip of international press coverage; the combination of remote indigenous communities, unique plants and animals, and one of the world's mightiest corporations was too good a story for the media to ignore. For the most part the coverage was cautiously favorable. In 2001, a *Wall Street Journal* reporter called our consultation efforts "unprecedented" in the country, attempting "a unique piece of social engineering." Similarly, the *Economist* wrote in 2002:

> Tangguh is about more than profits. It is a chance for BP to show that its much-trumpeted embrace of corporate social responsibility extends beyond the boardroom and into the boondocks. That is why the company has

sent scores of sociologists, anthropologists and other clipboard-toting consultants into bayside villages to listen and learn from its local "stakeholders." BP's base camp, a temporary set of wooden cabins, is dominated not by grizzled oilmen talking shop but by these new, Gap-wearing consultants, schooled in the language of "community development." [...]

But despite its best intentions in West Papua, BP's room for manoeuvre is limited. Indonesia's army sees its job as defending national assets, of which Tangguh is one. BP says that it will not need soldiers billeted on the site—it is training a community-based force to stand guard. What worries human-rights groups is that the company's talk of social responsibility may be blunted by the need to keep pumping gas if things turn ugly.

It was probably intended as gentle mockery, but I took pride in being one of those Gap-wearing clipboard toters trying to create a different paradigm for energy development.

On the Personal Front

I was an anomaly not just as an MBA working on social issues in a company of engineers, but as a young single woman. Most of my colleagues were married with children, happy to chat during working hours but eager to start their long commutes at the end of the day. My fellow BP expats were mostly career oilmen with trailing families who socialized primarily with one another in hotel restaurants and their homes.

Through a friend of a friend I found Jakarta's ultimate frisbee team, which attracted a wacky mix of expats and locals:

journalists, embassy staff, aid workers, executives in national and international companies. These new friends not only provided me with a life outside of work but in turn helped my work, as many of them knew the country for longer and from different perspectives than I did.

Prospects for romance were few and far between, but being in love with my job and my company was enough for the time being. I had plenty to think about; for example, I still hadn't figured out how to reconcile the lack of tenses in the Indonesian language.

"Budi, have you done that memo?"

Budi smiled. "Yes, Christine, I do memo."

I smiled, then frowned. "You *did* the memo, or you're *going* to do the memo?"

Budi smiled again. "Yes, I do memo."

This was getting silly. "Budi, may I see the memo?"

Budi nodded. I resisted the urge to strangle him. "Today?"

"Oh!" he nodded, then shook his head. "Tomorrow?"

My work was compelling, but it didn't exempt me from the day-to-day challenges of living and working in a foreign land.

Cautiously Optimistic

In 2002, as my two-year anniversary in Indonesia approached, construction was about to start on the new houses and the plant. It was time to bring in a new team and for me to start looking for a job elsewhere. The people of Tanah Merah had opted to split into two different sites a few miles apart. One hundred and one households chose the first site selected, prioritizing proximity to their ancestral land over water access and soil fertility; at least now they were making a fully informed choice.

Twenty-six households, most of whom were of a different clan, chose a different site a few miles away and closer to the water.

I came back to Tangguh in 2005 and flew over the new villages in a helicopter with Erwin. I pointed to what looked like a pile of corrugated tin behind one of the new houses; Erwin explained that some residents had built shacks to live in while they rented out their new houses to traders coming to the area from other parts of the country. I looked at him wide-eyed. Everyone's happy, he explained. The villagers like their new houses, but have realized how much more money they can earn by renting them out.

Despite some unexpected outcomes, on the whole I felt good about the relationships we'd established with the local communities and the partnerships we'd set up with other organizations. We had demonstrated that we would accommodate the community's interests whenever possible, for example by reorienting a jetty that would have crossed over a set of sacred stones and relocating another sacred rock to a bespoke shelter just outside the plant fence. (The rock was the size of a minivan and would have been too close to the LNG storage tank to be visited safely. The village elders invited Erwin to the ceremony where they asked permission from their ancestors to move the rock, chanting late into the night in a dark hut.)

There were still problems: jealousy among the residents across the bay, who did not have to relocate but felt entitled to benefits since the gas was closer to their shore; an occasionally recurring grievance that ARCO's seismic activity caused a 1997 measles epidemic that caused the deaths of four dozen children, despite an investigation that showed no link; and allegations of corruption among the third-party recruiters BP had hired, leading to new migrants getting jobs designated for original residents of the nearby villages.

Nonetheless, there wasn't the kind of violent social strife at Tangguh that is all too prevalent in extractive projects around the world—a relative success in the view of not just the company but external experts.

Michael Cernea, the resettlement expert, told me in 2013 that overall he was impressed with BP's planning and execution of the resettlement, though the company did not manage to avoid the common aid trap of dependency:

> Despite my initial skepticism, BP ended up producing one of the best Resettlement Action Plans that I encountered throughout my years, and achieved the fundamental objective: in the first and second years after the physical relocation, the incomes and overall livelihood of Tangguh's resettlers were clearly better than before displacement.
>
> What BP didn't do is organize the population so they will be prepared to manage the new assets and services introduced with the resettlement: the water supply, the power network, and so on. The idea would have been to create clear responsibility, to explain to everybody, 'We provide you electricity for the first year free, but then everybody will have to pay what they consume—at a very low rate but you have to pay.'
>
> Communities have to take over things and do their part because no project can assure provision of electricity into perpetuity. BP was good at building the new technical infrastructure for the village but were less equipped, of course, for promoting a social infrastructure.

In 2002, John Browne established the Tangguh Independent Advisory Panel to report directly to him "on how Tangguh can achieve its potential as a world-class model for development." Former U.S. Senator George Mitchell, who brokered the 1998 Northern Ireland peace agreement, served as chair. The panel's final report in 2009 read:

> Support for the Project is strong among both Papuan and local leaders. Although some complaints exist, there is near unanimous appreciation for the consultations among Papuans in which BP has engaged and for the specific tangible benefits that Tangguh has already brought to the area. Programs in the villages most proximate to the LNG site—the RAVs and DAVs [Resettlement Affected Villages and Directly Affected Villages]—have delivered improved health care, education, clean water, and economic development for the villagers.

Despite the success to date, there was also plenty of awareness that the way life would turn out for the people of Bintuni Bay was not in BP's control or even theirs. Whether Tangguh refuted or confirmed the resource curse would be the product of multiple factors, some more visible than others, that would play out over generations to come. Our efforts might prove useless or invaluable, but more likely they would never definitively prove to be one or the other.

Nonetheless, I left Indonesia optimistic about how business interests could line up with community interests. Even the most hard-nosed businesspeople at BP understood that an actively and constructively engaged community was critical to Tangguh's success.

I was also deeply grateful for what I had learned about multinational business so far, with all of its complexities and surprises. My experience with Tangguh bore little resemblance to the tidy, linear case studies I had read in business school. I was even more in love with my company than when I arrived in Indonesia, inspired by the commitment of my colleagues to make sure the company was, in a phrase sprinkled liberally in company statements and literature, a force for good.

Where could I go from there? Surely Tangguh was unique, in terms of the complexity of the issues and the resources that the company was willing to pour into them.

And then the call came—from China.

Chapter 2

CHINA: MAKING THE CASE

"Let's get started," said the manager to the assembled staff in the meeting room. With a trim black sweater over his button-down shirt, wire-rimmed glasses, and close-cropped hair, his appearance was as clipped as his manner. One of the translators repeated after him in Mandarin for his colleagues who weren't as comfortable with English.

The manager began running down the spreadsheet, the latest estimates for the cost and timeline to build a massive petrochemicals plant. BP was teaming up with Sinopec, one of China's state-owned energy companies, for this fifty-fifty joint venture that would bring a migrant workforce of ten thousand to fifteen thousand men into a town of thirty thousand residents. The area was surprisingly rural given its location thirty miles south of Shanghai, one of the world's largest cities (then with a population of around fourteen million) and China's commercial center. The man speaking was from Sinopec, but he wasn't the only construction manager; every major position had a BP counterpart so Sinopec could learn from BP's international experience.

"What's this?" asked Steve, the BP construction manager, jabbing a finger at a line in his spreadsheet that hadn't been translated into English. The other translator repeated his question in Mandarin.

"That's the number of projected fatalities," responded the Sinopec manager.

Steve's eyebrows shot up above his glasses. "Eight?!"

"Yes, based on the number of man hours over the two-year construction period and the usual statistics of a project like this."

"The target is not eight," Steve said. "The target is zero."

"But that's not realistic."

"Yes, it is. If you lower expectations, they'll be met. If we expect eight fatalities, there will be at least eight fatalities. The target is zero."

"That's not realistic."

The conversation carried on this way for a while. At first I was horrified that the Sinopec staff seemed so callous about the potential for multiple deaths on our watch. But as I watched them respond to Steve's challenges with statistics from recent projects, I realized that they were simply basing their judgment on their experience and knowledge of the industry. Were they right? Were Steve and I the ones who should be questioning our position? Was it really inevitable that people would die on this project?

My year working in China was spent bridging gaps between evidence and aspiration, what seemed real and what seemed right, Chinese and Western, Sinopec and BP. I was also learning the lesson that many Corporate Idealists confront early on: that the biggest challenge in pushing for higher standards is not winning over hostile activists or a skeptical media, but making the case to colleagues and business partners.

The joint venture was named SECCO, or the Shanghai

Ethylene Cracker Company. Ethylene is a petroleum derivative used to make polyethylene and polystyrene, the plastics that go into food packaging, toys, and countless other basic goods. With an annual production capacity of 3.5 million tons and a total investment of $2.7 billion, SECCO would be the largest ethylene producer in China and one of the largest in the world.

SECCO would be critical in supplying the world's factories. It would also be one of BP's largest investments in its thirty-year history in China, and therefore critical to ensuring that BP had a place in China's growing energy industry for decades to come. BP wanted to make sure that SECCO got up and running without a hitch, on time and on budget, and that it proved a good partner for Sinopec.

BP's head of China brought me to SECCO because he was concerned about the potential for problems with both the workforce and local residents. With regard to the workforce, risks existed both onsite and off. In 2003 China reported some seven hundred thousand serious work-related accidents and one hundred thirty thousand fatalities. Given the size of SECCO's workforce, the risk of such incidents was high, as our Sinopec colleagues freely admitted and seemed to accept.

One common cause of accidents was worker fatigue caused by excessive working hours. China has national laws on maximum working hours for construction workers that match international standards (eight hours a day, forty hours a week, thirty-six hours of overtime per month), but there are hardly any government labor inspectors to enforce those laws. Migrant workers, who leave their families behind for months at a time to earn wages that they can't find at home, often go along with demanding work schedules to maximize their earnings. Many don't want a day off, as they're too far away to get home and have little to do but play cards. Employers are happy to capitalize on their eagerness, but eventually working twelve- to fourteen-hour shifts with heavy equipment begs disaster.

BP had experienced construction managers like Steve who were going to focus on onsite safety, including working hours. But threats to safety didn't subside when the workers' shifts ended, which is where I came in. The men building SECCO would live in dormitories likely to resemble a cross between a fraternity house and a communist prison. The nongovernmental China Labour Bulletin reported that migrant workers in Shanghai dormitories had on average fifty square feet per person—about the size of a camping tent. At the worker dormitories I visited in the region to get a firsthand look at typical living conditions, I saw frayed hot pot wires used as laundry lines and rotting food stashed under bunk beds. Laura Rubbo, a senior leader in Disney's International Labor Standards program, told me she visited one dormitory in China where the women's bathroom had no toilets, just trenches, with standing water on the floor next to the only electrical outlets in the building where workers could charge their cellphones.

SECCO's potential problems extended beyond the safety of its employees. When working in remote areas, companies often build roads, water supply systems, and other critical infrastructure. SECCO's host town, Caojing, already had its own school, hospital, and sewage system, which eliminated some burdens for SECCO, but it wasn't clear that Caojing was ready to host the influx of new residents. SECCO's workers could drain Caojing's water supply, fill up the hospitals, spawn brothels (which commonly pop up near big migrant worker camps), and cause food and land prices to soar. Any of those outcomes might stir up resentment among local residents and party officials. China's industrial northeast was seeing a rise in citizen protests, which BP and Sinopec wanted to avoid.

BP recognized that such problems might jeopardize not only SECCO but BP's appeal to China as a partner for future projects elsewhere. A company might not have to take responsibility for impacts away from its site, but there was no question in this instance that BP would do so.

Outside the Fence

Other Corporate Idealists have seen how important those outside-the-fence issues are to the company and to workers. Jonathan Drimmer is vice president and assistant general counsel at Barrick Gold, the Canadian mining company. On his first day with the company in 2011 he flew to visit the company's operations in Papua New Guinea, where domestic violence is reported to affect two-thirds of all families. He realized on that trip:

> The problems with the community don't stop at your front gate. They don't stop at your doorstep. The community's problems are your problems. If you have extensive violence in the community, you have a serious risk of violence in your operations. Appreciating that you are part of and not distinct from the community, and their problems are your problems, is a mindset I didn't fully have before I went, but very much came away with.

On the positive side, Marcus Chung, now head of corporate responsibility for The Children's Place, told me that on his first overseas factory visit to Guatemala with Gap Inc. in the early 2000s, he was surprised that the factory owners had thought to build a bank, a grocery store, and other services onsite for workers. When Google and other Silicon Valley companies started doing the same ten years later, it was cynically seen as a way to ensure their employees never had to leave. But the facilities that Marcus saw were services that workers might not have otherwise had access to:

> They knew that they had a responsibility for the well-being of their workers. The bank allowed them to set up bank accounts, which many of the workers had not done before starting working with the factory, and they were able to start saving. For the factory, it would enable them to make direct deposit and reduce their manpower in terms of payroll and increase their efficiency; but it is a nice first step towards greater financial inclusion for the workers. And the ability to save, as we know, is the first step toward getting out of poverty.

Similarly, Elliot Schrage, vice president of Communications and Public Policy at Facebook, described the first factories he visited as a consultant to Gap Inc. in the late 1990s as "an engine of hope and change amid poverty. I was impressed by the contrast between the positive factory conditions and the appalling squalor that people were living in; and the remarkable difference between the living conditions of the homes of factory workers and their families and the homes where people had other employment or no employment at all. These factories were expressions of the opportunities for these communities rather than exploitation."

So hopefully at SECCO workers could realize opportunity rather than having their lives put at risk. I agreed with the company's business-driven position of risk mitigation, but as in

Indonesia I was interested in the moral case: it seemed obvious enough to me that BP should avoid causing social strife or harm, and should actually be one of those engines of hope and change.

Surely it was possible to get our business done without hurting people. Wasn't it? And surely our joint venture partners similarly wanted to avoid harm, even if they hid their caring behind a veneer of hard-nosed business drive. Didn't they?

As in Indonesia, I had the backing of BP senior management. But their moral support would only get me so far. I needed money for training, staff, equipment, and whatever else the changes I proposed would require, and BP didn't have full control of SECCO's purse strings. All costs were to be shared equally between BP and Sinopec; anything not written into the original joint venture contract had to be negotiated.

Typically, around the world in projects like SECCO, one construction company is awarded the job through a flat-rate bidding process. The managing company puts out a request for proposals; construction companies submit bids, saying they can do the project to the required specifications for this price; one company wins, and is paid the agreed price to get the job done. Workers have few advocates in China: there are few government labor inspectors, hardly any civil society watchdogs, and no real unions. So company owners often let measures to protect health, safety, and the environment fall by the wayside to leave more money for them.

Construction Company No. 10 won the SECCO bid. They would not take on additional tasks without additional payment, so any new safety measures had to be thrashed out with them and Sinopec, neither of which seemed receptive to anything that cost more.

Though workforce issues hadn't been a focus of my previous

assignment in Indonesia and I had no experience in China, the head of BP China thought that I had demonstrated the combination of business acumen and cultural sensitivity that SECCO needed. I was thrilled to be recognized in that way, if surprised that I was the only person he could think of with those qualities. Part of me wondered whether I was the only one naïve enough to accept this impossible assignment. But I couldn't turn down the opportunity to go to China, particularly to do work there that might help protect people.

I came to SECCO for three weeks in September 2002 to assess the situation. I spent the days getting to know people in the joint venture and the evenings meeting friends of friends and contacts of contacts to get a sense of how projects like SECCO typically played out in China. The old China hands I met were pessimistic that we could find common ground with Sinopec, but all were intrigued by BP's intent to install international best practices.

I eventually proposed a three-part plan. First, that SECCO establish its own health and safety standards for the dormitories and do its own audits, rather than the usual practice of leaving management of the dorms to the construction company. Second, that SECCO do a social impact assessment to identify and mitigate any potential problems with the surrounding community. The value of the study wouldn't be just the report, but the process of producing it: we would conduct interviews of local party officials and residents of Caojing, serving the dual purpose of establishing constructive relationships with our external stakeholders and engaging our Sinopec partners in doing so. My third recommendation was to hire a permanent Chinese Social Impact Manager. I estimated that these recommendations would cost a total of $840,000, practically a rounding error in SECCO's $2.7 billion budget. The BP executives agreed to support my plan, and told me that my next assignment was to convince Sinopec to do the same.

Making the Case

In the past China's companies provided lifetime employment, education, and health care, a phenomenon known as the "iron rice bowl." But after China began to liberalize its economy in the 1980s, focusing on growing exports and foreign investment, many of its companies began emulating their Western counterparts and shed such services. Now I had to convince Sinopec that they should reengage in the lives of workers and communities.

I needed to find the right words to build support for my plan. For the first few weeks, I tried presenting our goal as protecting the human rights of workers and communities. Contrary to popular Western belief that it's taboo or even dangerous to bring up human rights in China in any context, I simply met with blank stares. "What does human rights have to do with SECCO?" my Sinopec colleagues asked. (In 2013, the Global Business Initiative on Human Rights (GBI) held a conference in China, sponsored by the China Enterprise Confederation, the Chinese shipping giant Cosco, and Tsinghua University. Mark Nordstrom, Senior Labor and Employment Counsel for GE, who attended the conference, wrote in a blog post that "GBI member companies came away with the unanimous view that Chinese companies were more comfortable talking about business and human rights than any of us individually or collectively expected." But that was nearly ten years after I worked at SECCO.)

For the subsequent few weeks, I tried explaining that these were the standards BP used in its projects all over the world, but that fell flat as well. Sinopec wanted BP's expertise, but on its own terms.

I went into listening mode, trying to figure out what might resonate. I ended where I should have started, with an appeal to what seemed too obvious and clichéd to be effective: pride and reputation. The notion of "face" is a powerful motivator in China but all the more resonant in SECCO, as one of the Sinopec officials was rumored to have aspirations for the mayoralty of Shanghai. I peppered my slide deck for the SECCO board with phrases about "reputational damage" and "international best practice," and suggested that SECCO could be a world-class model project if we used the standards I proposed.

"Oh, yes," they nodded. "Why didn't you say so earlier?"

Talking the Talk

Finding the right language to make the case is one of the Corporate Idealist's most important skills. John Elkington, who coined the term "Triple Bottom Line" (referring to the three imperatives for companies of profit, people, and planet), wrote in a *New York Times* op-ed that when he began working with companies, "I often found myself envying James Bond. When 007 breaks into an enemy command center, he invariably seems to know which buttons to press. As I began to find myself called into more and more corporate boardrooms, I often had to press every button in sight to see what was linked to what."

Dave Stangis was the first formal corporate social responsibility professional at Intel and now heads sustainability at Campbell's Soup. He told me that the days of evangelizing are over: "We spent the first ten years of our careers, those of us that have been doing this for a while, to try to convince people they needed to be like us: they needed to think sustainability. They needed to think about corporate citizenship, reputation. Now you see us saying that's nice, but it doesn't work. You're not going to convince anybody. We have to help them do their job." Susanne Stormer, vice president of corporate sustainability for Danish pharmaceutical Novo Nordisk, told me, "It's extremely dangerous if we end up just thinking that we have to convert the whole world, because that is not how it's going to happen."

Liesel Filgueiras manages human rights and indigenous relations for Vale, the Brazilian mining company. She told me that a few individuals can block the railway leading in and out of a mine, so her operational colleagues are inclined to appreciate her work:

> In mining we are lucky, in a twisted way, because the impacts are very visible. The social license to operate is an ethereal and intangible concept for most companies. For us it is extremely tangible: it means stopping our operations.
>
> It's easy to make the case to say human rights is being able to operate. This is not hard at all, actually: I don't have to do a return on investment, I don't have to prove it. They know it. I ask them, "How much do you lose when we have our railway blocked for a day?" They do the math for me. It's extremely tangible.
>
> I work for the operations. I have clarity that if I do my job well, they will be able to operate well. It's not a short-term vision; it's a long-term vision because mining requires a long-term vision.
>
> When I talk to them on these terms, they understand. It's not trying to have them understand my language; it's talking on their terms and making sure that I'm not against them. I'm their ally.

I graduated in psychology and did my MBA in administration. I thought I'd never use psychology again, but 70 percent of my time I do because it's important when I'm posing resistance that they don't see me as an enemy. It's like, "Look, I'm doing this but I'm really on your side. You are your own worst enemy at this moment. What you are deciding is going to go against you in the long term for this reason."

In contrast to Liesel's finding common ground with her operational colleagues, another Corporate Idealist told me about one episode when a colleague of his in the social responsibility department failed miserably at winning over colleagues in other departments:

[My colleague's] pitch was, "One person can make the difference. Let's watch a video of Gandhi." I thought it was an odd choice for a business meeting, but thought, "You know what? Plus or minus, I'm actually on Gandhi's side. That makes sense to me."

And then she showed Mother Teresa, and I thought, "Well, we've got a broad section of pretty Christian folks. Mother Teresa, she's on the right side of history as well." But she lost the audience anyway.

You have to meet people where they are. There is no question in my mind that she is a very goodhearted person and smart, but she missed the thread that says, "This is how it ties back to you," or "This is how it's going to affect us."

Silvia Garrigo was Chevron's manager of Global Issues and Policy for four years, which included managing the difficult stakeholder relationships related to her company's operations in Burma and Nigeria and an ongoing legal battle over environmental problems in Ecuador. She told me: "In a company of engineers, decisions are driven by quantitative analysis and data as opposed to qualitative assessments and aspirations. Whenever I did get more impassioned about something, I noticed that I wasn't getting anywhere."

Silvia recounted a speaking engagement in October 2009 at which she got bombarded by hostile questions from the audience. As she was leaving the event, she received a call from her boss, Chevron's head of public policy, and the company's general counsel as they were reviewing the human rights policy that Silvia had drafted. Still reeling from the event, she was unable to keep her passion in check:

> They fired many questions and pushed back. To tell you the truth, they had legitimate questions. I had worked for the company for a long time but as a lawyer, where your job is not to build consensus but to advise. When you're on the business side, it's a whole other enchilada. I learned the hard way that I could not build consensus or drive progress with just passion and inspiration.
>
> My first reaction to all of their questions was, "Are we on the same planet?! I just got raked over the coals with questions on our commitment to human rights. If you don't understand why we need to get this policy adopted ASAP, you and I are not living in the same world." Every time they asked a question, I came back at them like they had thrown a Ping-Pong ball at me really soft and I'd slam and crack the ball with my paddle: "Take that, slam." I could hear this silence on the other side and I knew I came on too strong.

After I hung up, part of me said, "Holy __, what did I just do," and the other part of me said, "Well, whatever. It is what it is. They need to understand what I am hearing on the front line of these issues." Later my boss called me and said, "You came on a little strong." I said, "Yeah, I did," and I apologized.

What helped me is that I had a big bank of credibility with my boss and the general counsel. I had a number of other very constructive, thoughtful, and intelligent conversations with them where I was much more effective. I learned that it was not effective for me to be very passionate and forceful, that I had to calm down and be selective and more careful about my delivery.

Silvia's passion didn't completely backfire in that case: the human rights policy she drafted was adopted by Chevron two months later. Implementation is, of course, an ongoing process.

Translating Responsibility

I had secured funding from the SECCO board to move to Shanghai and implement my recommendations, but the hard work still lay ahead. I drafted standards for the dormitories based on BP's own standards as well as international standards like SA8000, a widely used standard for working conditions. I sent the draft to SECCO's translation department, who passed it along to the Sinopec construction team, who made their edits and passed it back to me through the translators. This process meant that the drafting took weeks instead of days, but I had to be patient: the Sinopec staff had to own these standards too, or they would never implement them.

During the editing back-and-forth, the Sinopec staff kept changing "smoke detectors" to "fire alarms." I had included separate clauses for both, but in every version I got back the two lines read identically. I rewrote the distinction into every round, but realized that I was demonstrating the saying about how insanity is doing the same thing over and over again and expecting different results.

I finally sat down face to face with the Sinopec construction staff to walk through the draft. I pointed out that "fire alarms" should be "smoke detectors." The translators translated, there was huddling.

"No, this is a translation error, these should be 'fire alarms,'" they said.

"No, there's a difference, and we need to have both," I replied. More huddling.

"This is beyond Chinese standard," they said, which was true.

"But smoke detectors save many more lives in case of a fire," I explained.

"This is not our responsibility, it is the construction company's responsibility."

"But if hundreds of men die in a fire in the dormitories, it is a big problem for SECCO."

"It is the construction company's problem."

"We can't risk that many fatalities, you know that."

"If this is so important to BP, then BP can pay for it."

They didn't hate construction workers; they were just being clear about their responsibilities, which they could hardly be blamed for. Their primary mandate was to control costs and they weren't budging, not even on smoke detectors that might have cost a few hundred dollars at most and saved at least as many lives. Despite the principle that all costs of the joint venture were to be shared fifty-fifty, there were items that BP was paying for on its own where agreement couldn't be reached, and we were clearly going to have to add smoke detectors to that list. I fretted about losing that round, but I hoped that my getting them to buy into standards at all meant progress.

Debating the appropriate allocation of responsibility is hardly exclusive to SECCO; all companies aim to minimize their risks and liabilities, which is perfectly sensible. But companies can't rid themselves entirely of the impacts of their business, even if they shift legal liability to a subsidiary or supplier.

The court of public opinion can enforce its judgments, as Nike found out in the 1990s when public outrage led them to allow independent monitoring of their supplier factories in Asia. In announcing the decision, then-CEO Phil Knight said, "I truly believe that the American consumer does not want to buy products made in abusive conditions." In early 2012, a *New York Times* exposé revealed harsh working conditions in the factories of Foxconn Technology Group, the company that assembles some 40 percent of the world's electronics, including many Apple products. The *Times* story sparked consumer boycotts, after which Apple joined the Fair Labor Association to have independent monitors inspect the Foxconn factories that made its products, and the two companies jointly committed to ensuring higher wages and better conditions. Three different Corporate Idealists told me, unprompted, that the *Times* exposé got them the attention and support from their senior executives they had been seeking for years: no one wants to be next on the front page.

In the cases of Nike and Apple, the public outcry took place primarily in the companies' home country, enabled by major media attention. In China, the media has not enjoyed the same freedom, which was made clear to us at SECCO. BP's health and safety manager on the project had arranged to bring his Sino-pec counterpart to a BP training course in the United Kingdom. Reviewing the agenda the week before, the Sinopec manager pointed to the session on media training.

"Why do we need that?" he asked.

"If there's a major accident," the BP manager replied, "the health and safety manager is often the one to explain to the media what has happened."

"But we wouldn't let the media know what's happened," the Sinopec manager said, puzzled.

BP didn't live in a world where companies could keep industrial disasters out of the press, but Sinopec did—or at least they had until now. We were sure that BP's international profile and SECCO's proximity to the lively Shanghai international press corps would render such anonymity impossible. That was fine with my BP colleagues, since the company had learned after being accused of complicity in human rights abuses in Colombia that transparency and stakeholder engagement were inevitable and even desirable. At SECCO, we faced a very different philosophy.

Getting to Know You

My BP colleagues were almost all men, mostly Britons and Americans in their forties and fifties. Two had married Chinese women and learned a little Mandarin, but for the most part the average level of knowledge of Chinese language and culture hovered somewhere around zero.

I did little to bring up that average, though my Chinese colleagues were tickled by my feeble attempts at learning Mandarin and seemed to appreciate my efforts, to the point where

I became a part-time English tutor. This was not in my job description, but allowed me to spend time with mostly younger staff who were eager to practice English, learn about the West, and talk about life in modern China. This was great fun for me; I had no one to rush home to and wanted to soak up as much of my adopted country as I could while I was there. I got more comfortable navigating the social dynamics at SECCO as I got to know people one on one, and hoped that these connections and my efforts to learn about their culture would reinforce my insistence that I wasn't there to impose Western standards on them, but rather to figure out what would be of mutual benefit.

These new relationships underscored my perception that many of my BP colleagues seemed to lack not just linguistic aptitude, but emotional intuition. SECCO's translators varied a great deal in terms of quality, and some of them seemed scared to deliver bad news. Even without understanding their words, I sensed that sometimes their pauses were due to something other than a lack of vocabulary. To me it was obvious when the BP and Sinopec staff were talking past each other, but everyone seemed to want to get through the meetings quickly and get back to their desks.

Many Corporate Idealists stressed to me how important it is to get to know people individually. One supply chain expert told me that she finally won the trust of workers she visited multiple times in Indonesia when, realizing that many of them were from farming communities, she brought photos of the farm she grew up on in Canada. "They couldn't stay chatting with me long enough!" she exclaimed. Monica Gorman told me that physically sitting with the production team when she was senior director of Corporate Responsibility and International Trade Compliance at American Eagle Outfitters helped her work: "I sit with Production and I've gotten to know people on a personal level; that really facilitates those tougher conversations. If we have an issue with a factory, knowing everybody and being here day to day, they come ask questions—'Do I need to audit this factory?' 'How long is this going to take?' They become more comfortable with the concepts and it's not so adversarial."

BP didn't list interpersonal skills as an explicit requirement for overseas postings, just experience and technical expertise. But I became increasingly convinced that the so-called "soft skills" were at least as important—and were in fact harder.

The cultural divide at SECCO was so wide that even my colleagues' best efforts fell short. After I'd been in China for a few months, SECCO got a new BP director, an energetic Scotsman with an impenetrable accent. He joined me and two Sinopec colleagues in the canteen and proceeded to regale us with—as far as I could tell—a detailed description of BP's brand new London headquarters, which he had just visited. He laughed at his own jokes, finished his lunch, shook our hands, and went back to his office. "What did he say?" my Chinese colleague asked. "I have no idea," I replied. We went back to our lunch boxes. Our new boss might have won them over in Aberdeen, but he wasn't winning any popularity contests in Shanghai just yet.

I soon found out that communications challenges aren't confined to individuals. When I first arrived in China, I was surprised to find that four years after the company officially changed its name from British Petroleum to BP, Chinese staff were still using the old name in conversation and written correspondence, and having their old business cards reprinted at local copy shops rather than ordering new ones from the company. I asked a few people why but got nothing more than giggles and shrugs in response, so I wrote it off to inertia.

Finally a friend outside of the company revealed that BP had fallen into an even worse trap than the apocryphal story about Chevrolet's Latin American launch of the Nova, which approximates Spanish for "no go"—not a great name for a car. With the wrong combination of context and tone, B in Mandarin can sound like slang for "vagina," and P like "fart." In the dialect of Guangdong Province, it can also mean "big pig." No wonder the new corporate identity hadn't caught on.

Along the spectrum of ways that a company can demonstrate insensitivity, this was more funny than egregious. But how good could it be for morale if people laughed every time someone said the company's name? The company and its branding consultant had held many focus groups during the rebranding. Did Chinese staff speak up? Were they ignored? BP wouldn't have had to abandon its preferred new global identity, just made sure that there was a better Chinese homonym.

A misstep on something so basic as the company name in such a major market made me wonder if human rights and the environment might be too complex to tackle.

Handover

The second part of my original three-point plan for SECCO was to conduct a Social Impact Assessment, which I commissioned from the Shanghai office of the international consulting firm ERM. Having learned from my experience overseeing the human rights impact assessment for BP in Indonesia that local expertise is critical, I had ERM's international staff partner with faculty from a public university in Shanghai. The social impact assessment team held a risk assessment workshop with BP and

Sinopec staff, met with local party officials, and conducted a survey of households in the area.

The main community concern was air pollution. Even though SECCO probably wouldn't impact air quality, the perception that it might was enough for SECCO to initiate discussions with the Shanghai Chemical Industry Park (the complex that SECCO was part of, with other companies building facilities at the same time) about instituting a public air-monitoring program, which was eventually established.

The social impact assessment was a good piece of work, well-written and comprehensive, though I thought its real value was in bringing Sinopec staff to the table to discuss these issues. The other benefit of the assessment was one that many Corporate Idealists mentioned to me: getting external voices to make our case. As frustrating as it can be, sometimes it is more effective to have an outsider make an argument that someone inside the company has been making all along. Such external voices can take the form of a study, an external advisory panel, or a single individual. One Corporate Idealist told me: "I established good relationships with a number of the folks in the socially responsible investment community and some NGOs, and have indicated on a confidential basis that a letter to a certain person or an e-mail on a particular issue could be helpful. Working with colleagues externally to help me move the ball internally has been a tactic and a strategy that I have employed."

The third and final part of my plan for SECCO was to recruit a Chinese social impact manager, since as an expensive expatriate who didn't speak Mandarin (and wasn't likely to anytime soon) I was not a sustainable solution. I wrote up a job description, explaining that the position included engaging the local community and ensuring good working conditions. Our

Human Resources Department posted to their usual recruitment sites and within days we had received a dozen applications. However, my excitement was dampened as soon as I glanced at them: the few cover letters that even mentioned the job title simply repeated the job description, à la Miss America ("I want to be SECCO's Social Impact Manager to manager [sic] the SECCO's social impact"), and most were from engineers who I suspected automatically applied to any position with BP or Sinopec or any chemicals company. The job description clearly stated that fluency in English was a requirement, but many of the applications were barely coherent. None of the applicants had any experience working on anything even tangentially related to dormitory standards, workers' rights, or community issues.

After a few weeks of increasing despair, one of the Sinopec staff referred Jenny Liu, a Beijing native who had worked for both government and multinational companies, and was one of a very small number of applicants who understood what the position was about. Jenny was just over five feet tall, wiry, with shoulder-length hair and piercing eyes, quick to ask questions but equally quick to stop talking and listen. I had found my successor.

By the summer of 2003, I had completed the three-point plan that I was brought in to execute. Construction was well underway, the dormitories were safe, the social impact assessment was complete, and we had established good relationships with local officials and communities. Local residents occasionally voiced concerns about pollution, but Jenny handled them with great skill and respect, inviting them in to tour the site, explaining what the various parts of the facility did, and letting them know what they could expect to see and hear. Jenny later told me that Sinopec staff were wary of her when she first came on board, but they always had her present when government ministers and other VIPs came to visit the facility—a sign of true respect.

I found a new job with BP's corporate planning team in London and left Shanghai in August.

Levers

In 2005, SECCO celebrated its opening with a lavish ceremony. There were no fatalities on site during construction, though there was one road fatality off site involving a SECCO vehicle. I never saw the official incident report but heard that the victim was a farmer pulling a cart across a new two-lane highway, taking the same route he had taken for years before the road was built.

Despite that tragedy, no major construction accidents on a project as big as SECCO was considered an achievement. The construction workforce had dispersed to their next projects, and there hadn't been any community problems with their presence.

In fact, Jenny proved so adept at her role that a European company building a similar facility nearby hired her away soon after I left, and SECCO didn't replace her. I was frustrated when I heard the news, but we had made it through the risky construction phase mostly unscathed.

A few years after I left Shanghai, I found myself on the BP China website, clicking on a page boldly titled, "The Triple Bottom Line of SECCO." The page cites SECCO's number-one ranking by the China National Bureau of Statistics for most efficient enterprise among basic chemical raw material manufacturers, pointing out that "Other than economic profits, sustainability and innovation capabilities were also critical to the ranking." The page goes on to describe SECCO's deputy general manager as being "overjoyed" to receive the award, as he recalled that "No accidents, No harm to people, No damage to the environment" was the mantra adopted at SECCO's first board meeting.

The same website also highlights the Social Impact Assessment, undertaken "to make sure that the construction is well accepted and can also benefit the local community." In 2013 I got back in touch with Jenny, who continued to work in corporate social responsibility for Western companies in China after she left SECCO. She told me that for all of the growing attention paid to workers' rights in China, the attention that we gave to the surrounding community made SECCO "the pioneer in China. For that I'm still proud of BP even now."

Pride is indeed a powerful motivator in China. According to Jenny, SECCO became a model of responsibility within Sinopec; even the Sinopec staff who were skeptical of the work we did at first became proud of their exemplary status.

With other multinational extractive companies like Shell also promoting corporate responsibility practices in their China projects, Sinopec was bound to follow suit. Sinopec did indeed establish a Corporate Social Responsibility department; in 2011 its chairman, Fu Chengyu, joined the board of the United Nations Global Compact, the world's largest CSR initiative. Hundreds of corporate sustainability reports are now published by Chinese companies every year, and the Shenzhen and Shanghai Stock Exchanges require their listed companies to report on social issues.

Not everyone believes that company efforts are the solution for Chinese workers. William Nee works for China Labour Bulletin, a twenty-year-old NGO based in Hong Kong. He told me that their executive director reached out to a number of brands manufacturing in China in the early and mid 2000s about piloting worker committees to engage in collective bargaining, but none responded. Since then, they've focused instead on collaborating with workers to understand and exercise their rights and have seen some success. William believes that the shrinking of China's workforce (today's workers are products of the one-child policy) and the country's aspirations toward higher-end manufacturing will force better treatment of workers:

> Ten years ago, there was the impression that there was an endless supply of workers from the countryside; if you went into a train station in China in the mid 2000s it was unbelievable how many people were coming in. There was the impression that you can fire whoever you want and tomorrow you can open up the door and there will be new workers. But that is clearly not the case these days: a lot of factories have to go deep into the hinterland and hire labor agencies to find enough workers, and these workers are much more aware of their rights.
>
> As Chinese factories are trying to upgrade, a lot of the workers will have higher skills and won't be as replaceable. It will definitely be in a company's best interest to have better policies and better labor relations.

It may be in a company's best interest to support workers' rights, but depending on companies strikes William as paternalistic:

> The CSR message is slightly disempowering. Because it is, "Oh, these people are working in such terrible sweatshops." You put the emphasis on how terrible it is and how helpless they are, and then you say, "But *you*, as

a consumer in the West, have the power through your purchasing to improve conditions by putting pressure on the brands. Tell Apple or tell whoever that they need to improve conditions and not buy from sweatshops. Save them, these poor people."

As a consumer I don't want to buy products that were made in terrible conditions or slave labor, so I understand that message. But our long-term goal is to see a democratic China, to see citizens rise up and not have a bloody revolution and overthrow the party with pitchforks, but to have a peaceful transition toward something better.

If one-third or 20 percent or even 10 percent of China's workforce is engaging in collective bargaining, meaning that they have democratic workplace elections and hold their worker representatives accountable when they negotiate a bad deal, and if they are able to have principled dialogue with the companies and engage in bargaining based on the principle of mutual compromise, if that takes place in China, China will become a democracy.

William told me he is also optimistic because the Chinese government is becoming more responsive to workers' needs, which echoes developments outside of manufacturing. In response to unrest around major projects both at home and abroad (for example, Zambian workers were shot at a Chinese-run mine in 2006 after protesting labor conditions), the Chinese government established partnerships with the British and Swedish governments to conduct corporate responsibility training. In 2012, China's State Council ordered that all major industrial projects in China must complete a "social risk assessment with stated project impact mitigation schedules." There is still a tragic abundance of worker abuse and pollution, in China and with Chinese enterprises abroad, but there is also a growing body of evidence that corporate social responsibility is slowly being embraced.

China's version of responsibility won't be a mirror image of what it is in the West. Even though Jenny was fully on board with promoting international standards for the dormitories in SECCO, she felt that we had to make concessions to local conditions. For example, BP standards called for hot running water in the dormitories, but Jenny pointed out that few families in the area had hot running tap water. Eventually SECCO installed hot water in the showers but not the taps. "Ultimately, the good standard means the best standard at the local environment," she told me years after our time at SECCO. "You can't have a real, single, valid standard all over the world."

On the contrary, human rights standards are supposed to be universal. But having had to translate such standards into operational realities in different countries, I take Jenny's point.

Again, the main audience for that translation is often one's own colleagues. Gillian Davidson, director of social responsibility for Canadian mining company Teck Resources, told me that having to focus so much on her colleagues rather than the company's external stakeholders surprised her: "When I came into the organization, one of my biggest learnings was how much I actually had to turn a full 180 and look inside. I had to spend 80 percent of my time in the beginning looking internally into the organization, and treat it like a community of interest. And I can apply all the same techniques that you would in working with an external community. I did not expect that."

Anna Murray is founder of the group Young Women in Energy and was previously with the mining company GlencoreXstrata. She told me, "I definitely have had times where I felt completely defeated because you're building towards what you consider to be high impact activities—only to come up against your own team members. It's not like you are competing against a misdirected statement in the media or a disgruntled NGO. That's the irony of the entire job: the biggest challenge and push back can sometimes come from your internal stakeholders."

Making the case does not always mean making an economic argument. Sometimes a dollars-and-cents approach works, but some argue that relying on "the business case" actually undermines greater respect for people and the environment.

Sir Geoffrey Chandler, a former senior executive at Shell who founded the Amnesty International U.K. business group, was one of the most outspoken proponents of this view. In a 2001 speech, he said of the business case:

> It is a rationalisation, not a justification. It is nothing to do with right and wrong. Indeed it is wholly devoid of any concept of right and wrong. It argues that ethical behaviour has to be justified by its financial reward. Sure, we all use it to sustain our arguments. But we need to recognise that it is fundamentally an amoral concept: it argues that a company should not do right because it is right, but because it pays. It may indeed pay, though it is casuistry to argue that reward always follows. And historically business has argued that doing right—whether ending the slave trade or protecting the environment or, more recently, introducing a minimum wage—would not pay. Moreover the 'business case,' unlike principle, is an impossible guide to the many decisions that a manager faces in real life.

Principle and profit are of course not antithetical... But unless principle precedes profit—in other words you don't accidentally kill or poison people in your employment because it's bad for business, but because it's wrong—public suspicion of business is understandably reinforced. Moreover, people will go on being killed and poisoned. Indeed, there is an arguable business case for bribing, lying, and polluting if you can get away with it, as many have and can and do and will.

It seems ludicrous to have to make a financial justification for preventing harm to people. But I also know how important it is to have one's assumptions challenged from time to time, and to approach work with humility and an open mind. Susanne Stormer, vice president of corporate sustainability for Danish pharmaceutical Novo Nordisk, told me, "I don't look for harmony because harmony is like a still life. When you have opposition, that helps you. It helps you sharpen your argument; it helps you reflect about who you are and where you're coming from; and it makes you think, I have to do a better job at listening to them to understand where we may find common ground."

Anna Murray of Young Women in Energy told me: "It's hypocritical because I sometimes resent these operations guys coming into these meetings with their goals and bias, and yet I come in doing the exact same thing. I think because my priorities are for the 'greater good of humanity,' they should carry more weight. I think, 'You guys should be as enlightened as I am.' It's such an arrogant and arguably out-of-touch place to come from." Corporate Idealists have to find common ground with their colleagues and business partners, which might mean using different language or metrics than what they first had in mind, without losing sight of their ultimate goals.

The way in which business is conducted and talked about is shaped in large part by a company's leadership. In my next role in BP's headquarters, I would see this firsthand.

Chapter 3

LONDON: TONE AT THE TOP

The final stretch of my new commute took me through the upscale shopping arcades of Mayfair, the central London neighborhood that for a while was the most expensive property on the British Monopoly board. The area is home to the city's and increasingly the world's wealth, originally from its residents and now from the hedge funds and real estate firms that make their home there.

In 2002, the year before I moved to London, BP moved its headquarters from an imposing Baroque stone building near London's financial center to an elegant neo-Georgian property in St. James's Square, also home to respected international affairs think tank Chatham House, the London Library, and the East India Club, founded as a civilized refuge for officers of Her Majesty's Army and Navy.

The walk put me in the right frame of mind for entering my new work environment. I was now at the heart of a company that traced its roots back to 1908 and was as much a part of Britain's history as Winston Churchill. In 1914 Churchill, then first lord of the admiralty, lobbied Parliament to buy a substantial share of what was then the Anglo-Persian Oil Company, eventually to become British Petroleum and then BP.

Despite being at one of the centers of history and power—for my company and for the world—I had mixed feelings about moving to London. There are worse places to be, for sure, but both the city and the job I moved for seemed to hold far less potential for exotic adventures and eye-opening experiences than my previous three years in Asia.

But I needed more exposure to the company's senior executives and greater fluency in financial and commercial language, which was at times more foreign to me than the Mandarin I failed to master in Shanghai. I needed that fluency both for my own credibility within the company and to be able make a compelling case for social issues, which I assumed I would continue to advocate for whether or not they comprised my full-time job. How much money could we lose by not talking to local communities, for example through having to pay extra security costs to protect our staff and assets against angry mobs, or delaying project start dates because our roads were blockaded or equipment sabotaged? My time in China and all that I had learned so far about corporate responsibility had imbued me with healthy skepticism about "the business case," but it was the language of the company and therefore what I needed to be able to speak.

There were a few examples of failure to manage "above ground risk" that came with dollar figures, such as ExxonMobil's four-month shutdown of its Aceh operations in 2001 due to civil unrest, which was estimated to have cost the company $100 million to $350 million. But even without precise costs there were plenty of other draws on resources, like the diversion of staff time and reputational damage.

While the risk mitigation argument seemed compelling, it was hardly inspiring. Framing it in positive terms, how much money can a company earn and how much value can be created by handling human rights well? New studies regularly emerge correlating good sustainability practices with good financial performance, but I have yet to see one that clearly shows causation. There is rarely a direct link between corporate responsibility investment and financial performance; there are too many other factors at play, like market conditions and competition. In 2008, the International Finance Corporation began developing a tool that aims to calculate a probable range for the net present value of investments in sustainability, but it is still more art than science.

So I knew I wasn't heading toward a magic formula. But I still felt like a little more analytical rigor would do me good, and I was looking forward to experiencing life in the company's nerve center.

In the Mothership

Behind BP headquarters' understated exterior was a modern, open environment. Staircases that would have suited M.C. Escher crossed each other in the central atrium. The building had every amenity, from a webcam pointed at the queue in the lunchroom so busy executives could minimize their waiting time (rumored to be the most popular company intranet site in the United States, I guess for employees to check out their U.K. bosses) to yoga classes at 5:30 p.m. on Mondays.

The building's luxury masked the tensions that it housed. There was ongoing competition between the main businesses: Exploration and Production—finding resources and getting them out of the ground; Refining and Marketing—converting them into products and getting them to market; and Gas, Power, and Renewables—developing resources other than oil. The competition was in part over resources; BP had a fixed amount of capital to invest every year, to be allocated where it would generate the highest return or strategic benefit for the company. Capital expenditure for Exploration and Production dwarfed all else—$10.1 billion in 2005 compared to $2.6 billion for Refining and Marketing and a mere $235 million for Gas, Power, and Renewables—but every project still had to be justified.

But the competition was also personal: the division heads—most prominently Tony Hayward, who ran Exploration and Production, and John Manzoni, who ran Refining and Marketing—were jockeying to succeed CEO John Browne, who was expected to retire within a few years. Staff lined up behind the candidate they thought would win, as they do in any company. Ed Potter, director of global workplace rights for The Coca-Cola Company, told me he sought opportunities to start briefing Mukhtar Kent about his work on labor rights long before Kent became CEO in 2009. Charlotte Grezo, who has worked at BP, Vodafone, Centrica, and Lehman Brothers, told me that she learned to "look at the politics and who mattered and who were the rising stars, and who did you need to convert for the future."

Other dynamics in headquarters included the operational types who were reluctantly putting in their time in headquarters in order to win a more senior position out in the field, and the older secretaries and functional staff who had been with the company for decades and were impressed by very little. (Some recounted to me the era when the tea lady would come around with a trolley every afternoon with settings appropriate to one's station. Senior executives would be presented with a tray with a cup, saucer, individual pot, and biscuit, while junior staff were handed a cup filled from a big urn. No matter how senior one wanted to be, the tea service didn't lie.)

The main players were the vice presidents and above, mostly British men in their forties and fifties, and a more international group of younger high-flyers doing one- or two-year stints as their assistants. The latter were known to all as turtles, after one late night when a few of them decided they were as inventive and indispensable as the cartoon Teenage Mutant Ninja Turtles. At first I thought this a cute way to lend self-deprecating dignity to what seemed to be a bag-carrying job. But in return for a bit of grunt work, the turtles were exposed to how big decisions are made and how the higher-ups functioned. Hayward, Manzoni, and Bob Dudley (who would go on to run the Russian joint venture TNK-BP and then BP after Hayward) had all done stints as Browne's turtles, and in turn their turtles had gone on to run major business units within the company.

As part of the corporate planning team, my job was to pull together data from the various businesses to help the top executives analyze the company's performance as a whole and determine capital allocation for the years ahead. But I was reminded of what I had learned in Indonesia, that spreadsheets were not my calling. Thankfully within a year Nick Butler, the group vice president for strategy and policy development, whom I had worked for during my summer internship in 1999, asked whether I might work with him again, as he had a great deal of work to do and no staff.

Some colleagues advised me not to take the post, to keep struggling with spreadsheets in a "real" job instead. But I was gaining clarity on my strengths and passions, and realized that there might have been hundreds of people in the company who were better analysts than me, but not a dozen who were better suited to a policy role. As I looked around the company, Nick's portfolio was the only one that was relevant to the stories I was drawn to in the news or what I read in my free time. I was less interested in the internal workings of the business than in its externalities, namely its impacts on its host communities and countries beyond direct employment and tax revenues. Even friends outside the company who shared my commitment to social change suggested that I would eventually be better placed to lobby for the issues I cared about if I set them aside while working toward more senior mainstream roles. But I didn't want my social justice muscles to atrophy, and could see that BP needed more people to focus on its externalities today—as did the communities living near its projects.

Human Rights

So in the summer of 2004 I happily fled Excel and dove back into Word, preparing briefing papers for Nick Butler on geopolitical issues and filling in data for speeches he drafted for himself and John Browne.

In January 2005, the two of them traveled to Davos for the World Economic Forum's annual gathering of the world's power brokers. Browne sat on a panel entitled "Does Respecting Human Rights Pay?" It was not one of the mainstage Davos panels for which attendance was strictly controlled but part of the Open Forum, a series of events open to the activists who showed up every year to protest the negative effects of globalization and the disproportionate power of the elite. Browne spoke earnestly of BP's initiatives to invest in the communities around its facilities. He was followed by a Nigerian preacher who had spent years campaigning against Shell in the Niger Delta and had little confidence in corporate goodwill. Next to speak was Irene Khan, then-secretary-general of Amnesty International, who urged that corporations be held accountable for human rights under international law. By the applause and cheers, the audience seemed to agree that voluntary initiatives like those of BP weren't good enough.

Browne rarely got flustered, but seemed taken aback by the ferocity of this debate. He believed that BP acted in good faith, contributing to communities' well-being, particularly in places where the government was failing to do so. But others thought that the human rights impacts of international business merited much closer attention by lawmakers and regulators. Browne described how BP's code of conduct was so well-enforced that 190 employees had been dismissed the previous year for breaches. But that was irrelevant to the audience, who wanted to hear about corporate legal accountability for human rights abuses; Browne's statements that human rights were about respect and dignity sounded like platitudes to the angry crowd. His position only worsened when one antagonistic audience member asked Browne his salary as a demonstration of how out of touch he was with the communities he was talking about. Browne answered truthfully—about £1.4 million base (about $2.5 million U.S. at the time, which probably put him in the lowest income bracket of Davos attendees)—and was met with loud boos.

After the panel, Browne stepped off the dais and said to Nick, "We need clarity on our position this year."

Nick recounted all of this to me when he got back to London. To him the Davos conversation was yet another example of the growing pressure on BP to define its values, and indeed on all companies to keep pace with a world of changing expectations. Nick instructed me to find out what was going on in the debate about business's responsibilities for human rights and determine what we needed to do. I had my assignment for 2005, excited to have a meaningful project that came directly from the CEO.

I started researching how people were talking about business and human rights both inside and outside of BP. One of the major oil and gas industry associations had just established a human rights task force, since many of our peer companies were facing serious problems: ExxonMobil was named in a lawsuit alleging complicity in human rights abuses in Aceh that would wend its way through U.S. courts without resolution for more than a decade; with its 2001 merger with Texaco, Chevron acquired a long-running dispute in Ecuador over environmental damage and was soon to take over Unocal's problems in Burma, where the military allegedly tortured villagers during the construction of a pipeline. A proposed set of standards on the human rights responsibilities of corporations at the United Nations was generating a ferocious public debate, which I would get immersed in before too long.

BP's big projects underway in Angola, Azerbaijan, and Indonesia were all attracting the attention of human rights activists. Their concerns ranged from whether we were employing and encouraging violent security forces, to whether migrant workers were shutting locals out of jobs and driving up land and food prices, to whether our revenue and presence were being used by corrupt regimes to strengthen their power and repress political opposition. These concerns all appeared to be valid, and all demanded answers that, to my knowledge, did not readily exist.

A Company-Wide Conversation

I reached out to my BP colleagues in Colombia, China, Indonesia, Angola, Russia, and other parts of the world where there were human rights concerns, and found that many of them were facing similar challenges. For example, in many places BP was required by law to deal with militaries alleged to have committed human rights abuses; and many of our projects were in areas where the government wasn't providing social services to its citizens, so the company was being asked to step in. My colleagues were having trouble defining the boundaries of the company's role: Where does the company's responsibility begin and end? How could the company influence the military's actions? If BP gave money to build a school in one village, could it stand by while jealousy built in the neighboring village, possibly creating tension where there was none before? If the company then built a school in the second village, what about the third village? And what was BP doing building schools in the first place?

I got enthusiastic responses from the colleagues I contacted. Riffing off Ronald Reagan's anti-big-government sentiment, the eight most dreaded words in the corporate world are usually "I'm from headquarters and I'm here to help." One Corporate Idealist told me that he calls his headquarters staff "shiny office people" and cited John le Carré: "A desk is a dangerous place from which to view the world." But far from being annoyed by my outreach, my colleagues were eager to work through these issues with others rather than trying to solve them alone.

In the meantime, BP experienced one of the worst disasters in its history. On March 23, 2005, an explosion took place at its Texas City refinery near Galveston, killing fifteen people and injuring more than 170. Needless to say, many of my colleagues in BP headquarters were consumed by the aftermath of the incident. But I look back on that time and realize with puzzlement and embarrassment that I was not one of them. The Texas City explosion was framed as an industrial accident—a horrific one, to be sure—but never as a human rights violation and therefore not part of my assignment.

Now it is painfully obvious that both the Texas City explosion and my lack of connection to it should have challenged my impression of BP as a responsible company in which I was playing a key role. Looking back on that time now, I suspect that I believed what I wanted to believe, having already invested years in this company that I had come to love. One of the key findings of the independent commission that investigated the accident was that BP "has not adequately established process safety as a core value across all its five U.S. refineries." Perhaps I subconsciously attributed the problems of Texas City to its heritage company, Amoco, rather than its parent, BP, where ultimate responsibility had to lie. I also fell into the common trap of erroneously viewing "human rights" as a developing country concern, one to do with weak or corrupt governments and indigenous communities, not unionized workers in wealthy nations. Whatever my thinking was at the time, the result was that I compartmentalized the Texas City tragedy and saw it as an anomaly; after all, I was working with so many other BP people from around the world who seemed aligned with my views.

Even if Texas City had forged a link between my work on human rights and the company's U.S. operations, would that have made a difference? Is there any chance that my engaging U.S. colleagues could have helped prevent the Deepwater Horizon explosion five years later? Could embracing the primacy of human rights and commissioning impact assessments and projects and programs accordingly—as I was part of doing in Indonesia—have made a difference in the Gulf of Mexico?

It seems like a stretch to assert that it might have, yet I would wonder for years after the Deepwater Horizon disaster. But back in 2005, while others in BP worked on the assets and issues in the United States, I carried on working with colleagues in far-flung countries.

In October of 2005 I went back to Indonesia to meet with my former colleagues, eager to hear how they were doing, share what I'd learned about human rights since I'd left two years earlier, and discuss how others in the company were thinking about similar issues. Back in the prefabricated trailers of the Tangguh base camp, I sat with the community affairs team. I spoke about corporate complicity, the notion that companies might not commit human rights abuses themselves but might contribute to abuses committed by others, like public security forces hurting people in the name of protecting company facilities.

Complicity had become a common topic of discussion in the seminars and conferences I'd attended in Europe, but I noticed that my Indonesian colleagues were staring at me blankly every time I used the word. I paused.

"What is the Bahasa Indonesia word for 'complicity'?" I asked Erwin, my former colleague and the community affairs team leader.

"*Bantuan*?" he replied tentatively.

"What does that mean in English?" I asked Marci, a community affairs liaison.

"Helping," Marci replied.

"Ah, it can be, but it can also be more passive," I said.

"How about '*kelibatan*'?" suggested Budi, the liaison for the villages on the north shore of the bay.

"What does that mean in English?" I asked Erwin.

"Being involved in," said Erwin.

"It can be both of those things," I said, realizing that what had become a buzzword in the West didn't have a good translation here. I asked Budi and Marci to stand up, and had them act out different forms of complicity: "direct" complicity—I give Budi a stick and he hits Marci with it; "beneficial" complicity—Budi shoves Marci out of the doorway so I can pass by; and "silent" complicity—I see Budi hit Marci but don't say anything.

"Ah," said Agus, one of BP's newest hires who had grown up nearby. "Is that like when the police came over to the camp the other day and wanted to use our boat?"

Yes, that's a very good example, I said, shuddering at the knowledge that some of the human rights allegations against ExxonMobil in Aceh had to do with the company providing equipment to the military. "Now let's talk about what we should do when that happens…" We discussed how such requests should be immediately documented and escalated.

Coming back from Indonesia, continuing my research, and realizing that similarly difficult situations were potentially present around the world, I thought it high time to bring colleagues together to discuss our common themes and struggles and develop global guidelines.

After a few months of preparatory work—getting a few senior executives to sponsor the workshop so everyone knew how important it was, interviewing colleagues to understand their needs, identifying the main questions and shaping the agenda, determining the right mix of attendees and external speakers, and preparing the all-important preread book with background materials—the day finally arrived.

I had shunned our usual hotel meeting rooms in favor of the

Westminster Boating Base, a nonprofit with floor-to-ceiling windows right on the River Thames, in the hopes of setting the stage for a literally enlightening conversation. The sun made a rare late-autumn appearance to shine through on my colleagues who had traveled from all over the world to be there.

After a round of introductions, I pointed out an imaginary line running diagonally across the room, and asked people to go to one end if they felt like BP was doing well on human rights in their country, the other end if they felt like we were doing poorly.

Mauricio Jiménez, BP's corporate affairs manager in Colombia, walked beyond the positive end of the line and wedged himself in the corner of the room. We were all surprised by this, as BP's security problems in Colombia in the 1990s still dominated most people's knowledge of our presence in the country. But Mauricio explained the work they'd done since then, building trust with local communities and creating a human rights training program for the military with the International Committee of the Red Cross. They had learned from the company's mistakes, built relationships with local stakeholders, and come up with innovative programs that were improving conditions there.

"What happened in Colombia ten years ago is so infamous now," he explained, "that no one knows how good our relationships are now with the local community and the military. The human rights training program that we helped seed with the Red Cross has become mandatory for all brigades in the country, not just in our area."

No one was surprised that Anton Mifsud-Bonnici, a BP policy advisor based in Russia, and one of our colleagues based in China stood in the opposite corner of the room, but all of us were surprised by their explanations. We all thought that BP had to tiptoe around the difficult issues so as not to offend those host governments. But Anton, a former U.N. official originally from Malta, and our China colleague both thought BP was being overly conservative. "BP has far more room to discuss human rights than we assume," said Anton. "We do more harm to our reputation by staying silent than we would by occasionally disagreeing—with respect and integrity—with what is clearly wrong, and supporting those who are in the right."

The exercise was an eye-opener, challenging our assumptions about BP in different countries and highlighting the common themes and local variations on our human rights challenges.

We walked through the thirty rights and freedoms in the Universal Declaration of Human Rights (UDHR) and talked about how BP could impact each and every one of those rights. Companies might impact some rights more than others depending on their industry and where they were operating, but treating the UDHR like an à la carte menu was simply wrong. As Chris Avery, founder of the Business and Human Rights Resource Centre, has written: "When it comes to human rights, companies do not get to pick and choose from a smorgasbord those issues with which they feel comfortable. The international community has declared all human rights 'universal, indivisible, interdependent and interrelated.'"

In Azerbaijan, BP had to grapple with one human right that might not have been among the most obvious: the right to freedom of expression. Four days before the 2005 opening ceremony of BP's Baku–Tblisi–Ceyhan pipeline in Baku, opposition parties held a rally calling for free and fair elections, knowing that international VIPs and press would be in town and it would be a good moment to draw attention to their cause. The protest was violently repressed by Azeri police. The media asked the head of BP Azerbaijan, David Woodward, what he thought of the government's actions. Woodward called the violence "unfortunate" and expressed support for the protestors' right to assemble peacefully, which provoked a rebuke from the Azeri president's chief of staff: "Foreign companies should get on with their business and not interfere in politics." But the next opposition protest proceeded peacefully, some said because of Woodward's influence; the *Economist* suggested that Woodward was the second most powerful man in Azerbaijan after the president.

Free expression wasn't even mentioned in the proposed standards for corporate conduct that the United Nations was debating at the time. But that was clearly an issue that BP couldn't ignore. It was also an issue that would come to the fore of the debate over business's responsibilities before too long, as Yahoo!, Microsoft, and Google would come under fire for complying with various governments' requests to censor blog content or search results or to turn over user information. It wasn't feasible to pick a subset of human rights for companies to pay attention to.

At the end of the two-day workshop, I was exhausted but excited. I felt as though we had started to build a community of people inside the company who would be able to call on one another when they were struggling with human rights–related issues around their projects. And much to my surprise, they had all agreed that we needed BP's position on human rights in one succinct document. Usually the last thing businesspeople call for is another piece of paper, but everyone agreed that it would be extremely useful to have such a document to use for staff training, and to share with NGOs, governments, and business partners.

I spent the subsequent months working with my colleagues and external human rights experts to articulate what human rights means for BP, collect examples and case studies, and prioritize actions that staff could take. The final product wasn't that much different from what I envisioned right after the workshop, which was modeled after a similar document from the mining company Rio Tinto. But as with the worker safety standards in China and the consultative processes I undertook in Indonesia, I knew that the process was as important as the content, and everyone had to take part in the drafting process in order to buy into the product at the end of the day.

The note went up on bp.com in March 2006, with the following introduction:

> This note explains what "human rights" means to BP, articulates BP's position on difficult issues involving human rights and our business, and provides guidance for our leaders and employees. [. . .]
>
> In response to a number of internal and external requests and the increasing intensity of the debate over business and human rights, this note serves as a human rights "lens" through which group activity worldwide may be viewed.
>
> Expectations of local communities, regional and national governments, international observers, consumers and shareholders with respect to the role of business in realizing human rights have changed in recent years. Particularly as our business grows in the developing world, we must be aware of those changing expectations, and make use of the many new standards, tools, forums, and other resources to continuously improve how we conduct our business.
>
> This note builds on our experience around the world in order to strengthen our ability to address these issues in a rigorous, consistent manner. It is written for BP employees, but can also be used for external communications.

In keeping with our group values and code of conduct, every leader in BP is responsible for understanding how his or her activities potentially impact human rights, and for ensuring that employees have the necessary awareness, tools, and license to act in such a way that minimises potential negative impacts on human rights and furthers our commitment to mutual advantage, respect and human dignity.

The note goes on to explain that to "support our analysis and management of human rights issues, we categorize them into three broad headings: employees, communities, and security," giving examples of issues that arise within each category. This explained to our management and staff that while "human rights" may not be the language of business, they could translate human rights issues into specific people to turn to; for example, if they encountered a "labor rights" issue, they could turn to their Human Resources managers. The note also included a proposed checklist for project leaders, which included commissioning risk and impact assessments and establishing procedures to investigate and report allegations of human rights violations.

Translation and Policy

The translation function is one that all Corporate Idealists play, particularly when it comes to human rights, a language rarely spoken in corporate circles. Monica Gorman, head of corporate compliance for New Balance, explained to me that her goal in introducing human rights is "trying to help people understand it's really just a different way of talking about a lot of the same things that we already do." Once her colleagues get comfortable with the language, she can then work with them on new initiatives.

Doug Cahn, who ran Reebok's human rights program for fifteen years, told me about developing training modules for factory audit staff in Asia: "Understanding how to translate culturally, and in words, a document that's based on [International Labour Organization] covenants can be difficult. We made entertaining presentations at quarterly management meetings that started with quizzes and fun facts. We wanted to make a discussion about the serious issues of labor compliance and human rights something that the production and audit teams looked forward to."

Dan Bross, director of corporate citizenship at Microsoft, told me that he often plays the role of translator. For example, as a member of the Anti-Defamation League's Hate Speech Working Group, he participates in discussions on civil liberties and hate speech, then brings his takeaways back into Microsoft to inform policies as well as product features, like being able to automatically suspend Xbox Live users who engage in abusive behavior.

The BP guidance note achieved the goal of translating human rights into company functions. But the document was a "guidance note," not a "policy," which meant that no one would be required to follow or even read it. Even before the Texas City refinery explosion in 2005 BP had begun reviewing all policies, which would result in the 2008 launch of a new operating management system that integrated standards on health, safety, the environment, social responsibility, and other issues into one management system. But in the meantime, no new policies, and my colleagues wanted something on human rights as soon as possible. The trade-off was that there would be nothing like the mandatory training and certification that was in place for our code of conduct. I was proud of the guidance note at the time, optimistic that it would help my colleagues who had asked for it. But I was preaching to the choir, and in retrospect might have had a bigger impact if the guidance note had the breadth and weight of a mandatory decree. The people at the workshop represented the highest-profile projects like Tangguh and the Baku–Tblisi–Ceyhan pipeline, but there were also risks in smaller projects. Joint ventures in Africa and Asia might be small enough to escape attention, but were operating in areas where there were likely to be thuggish security forces and discriminatory but common labor practices like firing employees who became pregnant or tested positive for diseases like hepatitis C. Nor did anyone from the United States attend.

But having staff attend a single workshop and even establishing a mandatory human rights policy would not, on their own, have necessarily prevented any disasters. Doug Cahn, formerly of Reebok, told me that the issuance of direction from headquarters is an important first step, but "no declaration by any CEO that I've ever known causes, in and of itself, a set of labor standards to be implemented." Writing a policy can be a long and involved process, particularly if it's done properly—which means involving the people who will have to implement it and getting external experts to weigh in as to what should be included. But getting the words right and posting a document on the corporate website are easy compared with implementation.

That said, for some Corporate Idealists, a policy is a critical tool. Dan Bross of Microsoft told me that his company's human rights statement enabled him to go to colleagues "and start the conversation at *how* we were going to make sure we were respecting human rights, without having to spend too much time debating the *why.*"

I hoped that the guidance note would help BP move past

the "why" on human rights toward implementation as well. But I would soon learn that the rest of the world was stuck at a similar point, of not yet having the succinct, consensus piece of paper that would allow everyone to move forward.

A Global Debate

As part of my research on business's responsibilities for human rights, I found the global debate converging around a Harvard professor named John Ruggie. Ruggie was appointed by United Nations Secretary-General Kofi Annan in 2005 to "identify and clarify standards of corporate responsibility and accountability for transnational corporations and other business enterprises with regard to human rights."

Ruggie started his mandate by having private meetings with companies, governments, and civil society groups. He came to BP and spent two hours with me and my colleague David Rice, interrogating us about our experiences, David in Colombia and me in Indonesia and China, both of us now working with colleagues around the world. Ruggie struck me as the classic professor—avuncular, charmingly intellectual, genuinely curious—and David and I went back to our desks impressed with Ruggie's pragmatic approach as well as his ambitions for his mandate.

A few months later, David and I headed to the United Nations in Geneva for a consultation Ruggie held on the extractive industries. We filed into the Palais des Nations and made our way through the maze of escalators and hallways to the conference room.

Ruggie took his spot on the dais and a U.N. official gave a few welcoming words. Ruggie spotted me from his seat and gave me a nod and a smile. I regretted having agreed to speak on a panel that day, unnerved by the grandiose venue and the crowd, which I heard had become quite contentious on previous occasions. I delivered my prepared remarks about my experience managing human rights for BP's Tangguh project in Indonesia, then steeled myself for criticism that I assumed would come about BP operating in such a sensitive environment.

But I need not have worried. No one cared about my talk; everyone was focused on a proposal that had been floated at the United Nations two years earlier, spelling out government-like duties for companies related to human rights. That proposal had been set aside by the Commission on Human Rights, much to the relief of the business lobby, which felt the proposal put an inappropriate burden on the private sector. But a few campaigners were still vigorously promoting the proposal with Ruggie in the hope that he would revive it, and representatives from companies and lobbying groups were expressing just as vigorous opposition.

Ruggie let everyone have his say, asking just a few clarifying questions. At the end of the day he stated his appreciation to everyone for taking the time to help inform him. I was impressed with how he managed to soothe the angry crowd and intrigued by this motley assortment of people who had traveled from near and far: Filipino indigenous representatives in traditional dress, British company executives in three-piece pinstripe suits, European campaigners with tattered backpacks.

A few months later, in early 2006, Ruggie issued his first interim report just as I was finishing the BP guidance note. The clarity of his report far exceeded that of other U.N. documents I had tried to read. Ruggie had taken these nasty debates and found clarity based on evidence and logic that seemed impossible to refute. In doing so, he continued to establish his own credibility and build trust among this very diverse group of stakeholders. It occurred to me that he was the kind of person I might like to work for someday.

Around that time, Nick started encouraging me to look for my next role within BP.

"You should really look for a commercial role," he said, echoing the advice others had given me. "No one rises in this company without having run a business."

"What about you?" I asked. He smiled and changed the subject. Nick started working with John Browne in 1989 when Browne led BP's upstream business, and managed to move with Browne as he climbed the BP corporate ladder. Nick certainly wasn't the first person to shape his career by hitching his career wagon to someone else's, but I appreciate that he intended to give me sage counsel based on what he had seen over the years.

Soon after that conversation I had lunch with Calli Webber, a BP friend who had just finished a three-year secondment to the World Bank. BP had paid Calli's full salary and benefits while she was on loan to a Bank project to examine ways to reduce natural gas flaring, and promised to have a job waiting for her when she returned. About fifteen BP employees were loaned out at any given time to government agencies or embassies, nonprofit groups, or industry associations. The exchanges were a way for employees to broaden their horizons and BP to give in-kind to worthwhile organizations while gaining valuable expertise.

It occurred to me that John Ruggie had been given no staff and minimal budget and support from the U.N., as is standard with such appointments; consequently, many of the appointees treat them as primarily desk-based research. Yet he seemed determined to have a big, positive impact on the world, and I wanted to help him.

I e-mailed him, congratulating him on his interim report

and letting him know that the BP human rights guidance note was out. I wrote that I knew that the U.N. gave him minimal resources to carry out his mandate, and he knew a bit about my experience and interests—would he like any free help? He wrote back five hours later from his BlackBerry: "YESYESYESYESYESYESYESYESYESYES."

I drafted a proposal for Nick, saying that John Ruggie's interim report was being praised by many as a sensible way forward, and that he was conducting his mandate with so much outreach and consultation that his reports would both reflect and shape expectations—and maybe even legislation—that would impact BP for years to come. Wouldn't it be a great thing for us to support, and given that I had corporate experience both in the field and in headquarters, wasn't I just the person to do it?

I gave the memo to Nick and we sat down to discuss it the next day. He seemed surprised; at the time I thought he was impressed by my initiative, but I wonder if he knew this was the beginning of the end of my time with the company.

"Let's start it as a part-time project," Nick said. "We don't quite know how it's going to go, and I still have work for you to do here." I wrote up a memorandum of understanding that John Ruggie and Nick agreed to, and I started working part time for Ruggie in April 2006. Some NGO representatives expressed concern about my secondment granting Big Oil too much access to him; he responded in an open letter about his work plan that "It is important to have someone on the team who has actually worked in a company. By the same token, I would be delighted if human rights organizations also were able to second an expert to support the mandate." (The NGO Global Witness later took him up on his offer, seconding one of their staff to develop recommendations for businesses operating in conflict zones.)

It was hard for me to imagine life getting any better. I had just moved in with the lovely English gentleman I'd started dating two years earlier. At work I was still amidst the buzz of headquarters, working with colleagues around the world on issues that mattered, while also contributing to a United Nations effort to make an impact on a global scale.

How long could this ideal state of affairs possibly last? About ten months, as it turned out.

Transition

In the fall of 2006, Nick resigned from BP to establish a new center on International Energy Policy at Cambridge University. It seemed like a terrific opportunity for him, but I was surprised that he left while his close ally and friend John Browne was still leading the company. At the time I had no idea that even bigger surprises were to come.

Not long after that, my boyfriend was offered a transfer from London to New York with his company. With Nick's departure and an increasing amount of my time spent on the U.N. mandate, I figured I could come home to New York, be in the same time zone as John Ruggie at Harvard, and be with this man whom I suspected would become my life partner.

My new boss was a BP executive whom I had known for years, though I had never been sure whether he supported my work on human rights. I feared that he wouldn't see the value of my U.N. work.

The day before our first formal meeting I sent him a memo explaining my role, and that I would be moving to New York to continue it since my partner was being transferred there. I walked into his office the next day with a copy of the memo printed out two pages per sheet and double-sided, as I always do to save ink and paper.

Seeing the small font, he said, "Gee, you really take this sustainability thing seriously, don't you?" I stared at him, not sure whether he was joking. He stared back at me. We were not off to a good start.

Next he said, "New York won't work." He went on to say that the office is small and out of London's sights, home to only a few investor relations staff and a visitor services team to organize board meetings and occasional senior visits. He doubted that I could be useful to the company from such an outpost.

I couldn't tell whether he was serious or just testing whether I'd stand up to him in the first meeting of our new working relationship. Either way, I had decided that my commitment to my relationship outranked my commitment to BP, and therefore I had little to lose.

"Let's start again," I said. "I'm moving to New York because that's where my partner will be—and where I will no longer be an expensive expat like I am here. If you pull me off this U.N. project, it will attract more negative attention than you want right now. So why don't we start from there?"

He raised an eyebrow, and I thought I saw a flicker of a smile. He asked a few questions about the U.N. work—which human rights NGOs and governments were involved, what they thought of BP, what I thought the implications of John Ruggie's work would be for our industry—and within half an hour we were discussing my move date. I don't know that I convinced him of the value of my work, but at least he was letting me continue it.

A few weeks later, I flew to New York with the man whom I would marry one year later. I settled into BP's New York office and continued to do some work for the company, but was spending an increasing amount of my time with John Ruggie on his U.N. mandate.

End of an Era

While I was transitioning into my new life in New York, major changes were afoot back in London. John Browne never married, and lived with his mother until she passed away in 2000. Browne later wrote in his autobiography that he realized he was gay as a young boy in boarding school, but fear of the prevailing homophobic social norms—in mid-twentieth-century Britain and then in the corporate world—kept him in the closet, including to his mother, until after she died. His sexuality was a well-known secret among the top executives of the company and those of us who worked with them. No one I knew seemed to care. But one U.K. tabloid felt differently.

The Mail on Sunday had purchased a kiss-and-tell story from a Canadian man Browne had dated. Browne took out an injunction to stop publication of the piece and the legal back-and-forth carried on for months, unknown to the public and most of BP. In a statement to the court, Browne responded to a question about how he met his former boyfriend by saying that it was while running in Battersea Park, then later corrected his statement to say that it was through an escort service. The judge decided that Browne's having lied meant that the story could run. It hardly seemed a logical argument, but the damage had been done. Within hours of the judge issuing his decision on May 1, 2007, the press swarmed the steps of St. James's Square and Browne tendered his resignation.

As he later wrote in his autobiography, Browne was surprised and overwhelmed by the thousands of e-mails and letters of support that he received after his resignation. A number of London's great and good wrote a letter to the *Financial Times*, wishing "to place on public record our support now and in the future for our friend John Browne and to thank him for his immense and unique contribution to business, the economy and to art, culture and the environment. We wish him well, stand by him and look forward to working with him in the years ahead."

Despite the affection showed to Browne by many immediately following his departure, his reputation as one of history's greatest business leaders had already been damaged. During the final years of his tenure as CEO, BP had a number of serious incidents: in 2005, an explosion at the Texas City refinery killed fifteen people and the company's biggest production rig was nearly taken out by Hurricane Dennis; in 2006, a pipeline corroded in Alaska and spilled more than two hundred thousand gallons of crude into the Prudhoe Bay area, and BP traders were accused of manipulating U.S. propane markets in a case that was later settled. These incidents were tarnishing Browne's image as well as the company's stock price.

I had some sympathy for Browne throughout all of these incidents. I knew how hard he and the entire building worked, trying to keep track of BP's activities, which at the time spanned one hundred countries and one hundred thousand employees. I saw (and sometimes contributed to) how thick the briefing books were that executives took home every weekend, and thought that a conglomerate of such size and scope must be to some extent impossible to track. But leaders were ultimately accountable for what happened in the company and set the tone for how people behaved—which would become even clearer to me before too long.

Tony Hayward took over as CEO and wanted to signal to

the financial markets that this was a new era, that the company's troubles were history and he was now fully in control. He would have to make some dramatic moves to distinguish himself from Browne—after all, he was also a lifelong BP engineer, British, lean, and soft-spoken in public.

Hayward started with visual cues, replacing the fine art in BP's offices worldwide with photos of oil rigs and multicultural teams of smiling workers in hard hats and goggles, and ordered the head office security guards' suits changed from beige to black. "They should just put a big bronze pair of testicles in the lobby," one colleague griped to me.

More substantively, Hayward stated his intentions to sell off the Alternative Energy division, which had been launched to much fanfare in 2005, and reenter the dirty, carbon-intensive tar sands business that Browne exited in 1999. One of my friends started calling the company "Beyond Depressing." The U.K. press was all over Hayward for trashing BP's green credentials, but he seemed undaunted. In 2009 Hayward explained his approach in a speech at Stanford's Graduate School of Business:

> We had too many people that were working to save the world, which sort of lost track of the fact that our primary purpose in life is to create value for our shareholders. How you do that, you need to take care of the world, but our primary purpose in life was not to save the world.

As Groucho Marx said, I resemble that remark. I was under no illusion that I worked for a humanitarian organization. But I saw with my own eyes that not much shareholder value would have come out of the Tangguh project in Indonesia or the SECCO project in China without some world-saving, and knew I had many colleagues who felt the same way. The people I got to know at Browne's BP talked about the company's mission as delivering heat, light, and mobility without a hint of irony. Browne himself wrote in his autobiography: "After all, shareholder value is not about returns and growth rates alone; it is also about how long a company can keep growing. The 'how long' means a business must invest in the societies from which it derives its profits to ensure that its customers continue to be there and that governments continue to renew its licence to operate. A business must be useful to society and be seen as such."

In contrast, Hayward concluded his Stanford speech:

> BP makes its money by someone somewhere every day putting on boots, coveralls, a hard hat and glasses and going out and turning valves. That's how we make our money, and we've sort of lost track of that.

Sure, BP couldn't be full of policy wonks and world-saver specialists like me; someone needed to get the stuff out of the ground. But boot-wearers should be world-savers too. To me it felt as though Hayward was framing social and environmental engagement as extraneous rather than essential, and I disagreed wholeheartedly. Part of the purpose of my U.N. secondment was to develop knowledge and connections that I would bring back into BP, but it seemed increasingly unlikely that there would be a senior-level audience for my new expertise. I was less committed to BP than to the vision of an outspoken progressive company, and in my eyes the two no longer overlapped.

I sensed that the new BP would be very different to the one I joined in 1999—and I loved the old one. It would take a few years for me to realize that companies that big can't change that quickly, and that "my" BP was hardly perfect. But at the time, the leadership change felt to me like a seismic shift. In the fall of 2008, I left BP to work for John Ruggie full time.

Leadership Matters

I saw Browne a few months after he left BP, when I was still based in BP's New York office and he came by to thank the staff there for taking such good care of him over the years. He had kicked his longtime cigar habit, and it showed: he had some healthy color in his face and seemed to have shed the heavy-lies-the-crown fatigue that weighed him down at BP. I thanked him for being such a role model; he responded graciously and with a smile, which had rarely been seen in St. James's Square.

For all of the criticism that Browne attracted, I still admired how he took bold stances that shifted the global debate about business's role with respect to climate change and human rights. He would eventually apply those same advocacy skills to the problem of homophobia in business: in May 2012 he gave his first public talk about sexuality in the workplace to an engineering firm's LGBT network. In June 2013 he wrote an op-ed in the *Financial Times* in support of a bill in the House of Lords in support of gay marriage, and shortly thereafter announced that he would be writing a book called *The Glass Closet:* "I wish I had been brave enough to come out earlier in my tenure as CEO of BP. I regret it to this day. I know that if I had done so I would have made more of an impact for other gay men and women. With *The Glass Closet* I hope to give some of them the courage to make an impact of their own."

From my short interaction with him in his post-BP life, he certainly looked more comfortable in his own skin. I would do my best to carry on the progressive elements of his legacy. Nor would I be the only one: Ann Hand, BP's former chief marketing officer, went on to lead Project Frog, a pioneer in green buildings. John Melo, who held a range of senior roles in BP from branding to e-strategy, became president and CEO of Amyris, developing biofuels and other alternatives to petroleum-based products. Jan Slaghekke, former chief of staff for the Alternative Energy division, did a turn as senior advisor to Vestas, the world's largest producer of wind turbines.

When one Corporate Idealist I spoke with experienced a sweeping change of management at his company, he said he was taken aback at first to be questioned about the company's approach to issues he thought were well-established. But he came to a much more positive view of the turn of events at his company than I did at BP:

> I realized that that's precisely what I was getting paid for: I was getting paid to push back and help educate—that was my job! Furthermore, an engaged executive who actually was willing to throw out my status quo unless persuaded—she would also be willing to throw out other status quos, which could help make breakthroughs and progress. My job was to influence and educate and harness that drive. What an opportunity I had!

If I had known that Corporate Idealist a few years earlier, maybe I would have stayed and tried to "educate" the new Hayward regime in the importance of human rights. But that seems as naïve as the impression I formed working for Browne's BP, that all CEOs thought progressively about human rights and the environment, which is why Hayward's moves were so shocking to me.

It is also worth bearing in mind that even having the support of the most progressive CEO does not make the Corporate Idealist's work easy. Beth Holzman spent nearly five years at Timberland as senior manager for CSR strategy and reporting under CEO Jeff Swartz, widely considered a pioneer and leading champion of CSR. She told me: "Working with Jeff was unique and I was very grateful for him as an incredible ally and champion for this work. But if you're not thinking about the supporting structure around him, then you're only doing half of your job."

I still mourn the loss of Browne's BP—namely the community of people inside the company who were innovating to improve the company's environmental and social impacts. But Browne's departure led me full-time into the U.N. mandate, which would prove just as seminal an experience.

Chapter 4

THE UNITED NATIONS: CREATING OWNERSHIP

When I stepped out of the van in the morning, the sweet smell of syrup transported me to a childhood visit to Hershey Park, where the ubiquitous chocolate aroma kept me giddy all weekend.

But now it was midafternoon, the cloying odor was nauseating, and this was no amusement park. It was January 2007 and I was on the outskirts of Cali, Colombia's third-largest city, infamous for its history as a hub of Colombia's multibillion dollar cocaine cartel. I was with my boss, John Ruggie, the United Nations secretary-general's special representative on business and human rights.

We were touring a bottling plant, part of The Coca-Cola Company's supply chain but independently owned and operated. After a welcome PowerPoint presentation from the general manager, we visited the unloading area where raw materials arrived, the bottling lines where glass was molded into the unmistakable silhouette of the Coke bottle and filled with the secret sauce, and the lab where we donned shower caps and slippers to watch samples being taken for quality control. The production manager walked us around the complex, pointing out to us in broken English what each machine did.

The next day we were driven to a sugar plantation, another wholly separate business. Our host was a white-haired, well-tanned man, who brought us to the veranda of the main house for lunch overlooking the sugar cane fields. Servants in tuxedos and white gloves brought out lamb chops on fine china. "There are no human rights problems here," he said, tucking his napkin into his collar. "The problems you read about are a creation of the international media."

Seeing his two-car caravan with tinted windows and armed guards parked a few feet away, I didn't dare steal a glance at John. Our host went on.

"We have excellent community relations here," he said, nodding to the waiter to refill our glasses of Coke. "I built a water park for the residents of the town."

This was not exactly what we had come to hear. In 2001, the United Steelworkers Union and the International Labor Rights Fund filed suit in U.S. federal court against The Coca-Cola Company and two of its Latin American bottlers, alleging that the companies directed paramilitary security forces to murder and torture leaders of the Colombian trade union Sinaltrainal. The case was eventually dismissed, but the "Killer Coke" campaign that started around the lawsuit lives on. As for the sugar plantation, slave labor was known to be a problem in South American agricultural facilities.

The Coca-Cola Company, based in Atlanta, didn't own the facilities in Colombia. Their business model around the world is to contract with local bottlers, sometimes multinational companies in their own right. The bottling plant we visited was owned by FEMSA, the largest Coca-Cola bottler in the world with $13.5 billion in revenue in 2007, compared to Coca-Cola's $28.8 billion the same year. FEMSA was not named in the U.S. lawsuit in 2001, but bought into the problem when it acquired one of the defendants, Panamco, in 2002.

When we visited, The Coca-Cola Company held a 31 percent equity stake in Coca-Cola FEMSA, the division of FEMSA that managed Coca-Cola products, and two seats on its eighteen-member board. Coca-Cola had a set of Supplier Guiding Principles, which stated that "we expect our direct suppliers to follow the spirit and intent of these guiding principles to ensure respect for all human rights," including the right to join a labor union and the prohibition of child and forced labor. But FEMSA had its own policies; The Coca-Cola Company could not force FEMSA to adopt its principles verbatim or implement them in a particular way.

How much influence a company can have over its suppliers and partners was one of the many issues that John Ruggie was examining as part of his mandate. He had been appointed in 2005 by then-Secretary-General Kofi Annan to clarify companies' responsibilities for human rights after many years of polarizing and ultimately inconclusive debate. Unlike some U.N. appointees, his mandate did not include investigating specific claims of human rights abuse. Nonetheless, he wanted to visit company operations to meet managers and communities affected by business to understand their thought processes and see conditions on the ground with his own eyes. "I'm genuinely interested in what makes these things tick," he later told me.

I was excited to accompany him. Since working for BP in Indonesia I had become fascinated with this sort of far-flung business travel. Itineraries like ours weren't in the *Lonely Planet* or *Frommer's:* We were seeing scenes that had a bigger social impact than any tourist destination and meeting people who were not performing but grappling with very real challenges, to which we are all connected through the globalized supply chain of our consumption. I had developed a travel bug long ago, but this line of work took me to places that I never would have been able to access on my own. I was getting to sites that few others would ever see, meeting people on the front lines of globalization, and working to improve people's lives—too good a job to be true.

John seemed even more excited to be there. At the bottling plant, he seemed completely taken with the production manager. They made for an odd couple, not sharing a common language, John in a slate-gray button-down shirt and neatly pressed jeans, towering over the production manager, who wore baggy overalls and a red FEMSA baseball cap. But they persisted in examining every piece of equipment, pointing and gesturing and nodding to each other.

I couldn't see how understanding which chute led to where would help develop global principles. Later I would realize that it was John's ability to engage with everyone he encountered over the course of his work that led to his success. As Pablo Largacha, Coca-Cola's director for global issues management who helped organize our trip, later said to me, "We were expecting a U.N. official on a diplomatic mission, but this was like a family friend visiting you where you worked. He was blending in, connecting, and made everyone feel at ease."

At the time all I knew was that my boss was enjoying himself, so I continued to lag behind John as he and his new best friend practically skipped around the plant.

The Business and Human Rights Debate

Traditionally "human rights" has been about what governments must and must not do. The Universal Declaration of Human Rights (UDHR) was created in the wake of the atrocities of World War II, which inspired the international community to articulate a set of rights and freedoms that all states would commit to protecting and fulfilling. The UDHR has thirty articles, encompassing both civil and political rights such as the right to life, freedom from torture, freedom from slavery, and the right to privacy; and economic, social, and cultural rights such as the right to a fair wage, the right to safe and healthy working conditions, the right to education, and the right to an adequate standard of living.

Since the UDHR was adopted by the U.N. General Assembly in 1948 business has grown in scale and scope, lifting generations out of poverty but also contributing to harm. In the 1970s, a group of clergy questioned whether churches were profiting from the Vietnam War by investing their pensions and endowments in companies that, for example, manufactured napalm. This led to the creation of the Interfaith Center on Corporate Responsibility (ICCR), a coalition of faith-based organizations that leverage their power as investors to engage with companies. In 1977 Reverend Leon Sullivan drafted a set of eponymous principles for companies operating in apartheid South Africa to promote equal opportunity. ICCR members filed a variety of related shareholder resolutions, urging some companies to withdraw from South Africa and others that they thought could effect change to stay there and adopt the Sullivan

Principles, all contributing to the global movement that led to the end of apartheid.

After the Sullivan Principles drew worldwide attention, other entities began paying attention to business's impacts on human rights—and more companies began to demonstrate why that attention was warranted.

The Organisation for Economic Co-operation and Development (OECD) issued the first version of its Guidelines for Multinational Enterprises in 1976, and the International Labour Organization adopted its Tripartite Declaration of Principles concerning Multinational Enterprises and Social Policy in 1977.

The same year, Nestlé was accused of aggressively marketing infant formula in developing countries, sparking a worldwide boycott that has continued for forty years. In 1984 a Union Carbide pesticide plant exploded in Bhopal, India, killing thousands of people and leaving many more injured. In 1989 the Exxon Valdez oil tanker ran aground, spilling more than eleven million gallons of crude in Alaska's Prince William Sound.

In the 1990s, as the Internet was speeding up the rate at which information traveled around the globe, Phil Knight of Nike and talk show host Kathie Lee Gifford were caught up in accusations of their branded footwear and apparel being made in sweatshops in Asia and Central America respectively. Then-President Bill Clinton convened leaders from industry, non-governmental organizations, and universities (that purchase so much sportswear) to develop a code of conduct, resulting in the Fair Labor Association being incorporated in 1999.

While the apparel industry was wrestling with its social responsibilities, the extractive industries were on a parallel journey. In 1995 Nigerian writer and environmentalist Ken Saro-Wiwa was convicted of treason and hanged by Nigerian authorities along with eight of his peers after protesting

Shell's operations in the Niger Delta. Around the same time, BP was accused of hiring mercenaries to protect its operations in Colombia. The realization that there were no clear rules for how extractive companies should design appropriate security arrangements in difficult environments led those companies and others to work with human rights groups and the U.S. and U.K. governments to draft the Voluntary Principles on Security and Human Rights, which were launched in 2000.

By the early 2000s, a number of efforts were emerging to address particular issues in particular industries. But there was still no clarity on the fundamental underlying question: What are the human rights responsibilities of companies, no matter what they do or where they operate? Companies should not have the same duties as governments, since they are established for a specific function and are legally accountable only to their owners. But they clearly can impact human rights, so what are their responsibilities toward them? The preamble of the Universal Declaration of Human Rights says that "every organ of society" has a responsibility to promote human rights and "to secure their universal and effective recognition and observance," but that does not provide any guidance on what a company must do.

The United Nations

There is one organization that is meant to establish global, authoritative principles that all nations of the world sign on to uphold: the United Nations. But again, the U.N.'s core documents have always been negotiated by and meant for governments. Could the U.N. incorporate companies into what it does? Early attempts suggested no: the U.N. Commission on

Transnational Corporations was established in 1973 to establish a corporate code of conduct, but after many drafts was dissolved in 1994.

In 2003, a subcommission of the U.N. Commission on Human Rights presented a proposal entitled *Draft Norms on the Responsibilities of Transnational Corporations and Other Business Enterprises with Regard to Human Rights*. It should have been obvious from the name alone that the *Norms* wouldn't see widespread uptake.

But the title wasn't the only problem with the document. The *Norms* asserted that business has "the obligation to promote, secure the fulfillment of, respect, ensure respect of, and protect human rights"—in other words, that companies had all of the same duties for human rights as governments. The *Norms* provoked a strong negative reaction from the International Organization of Employers and the International Chamber of Commerce, who asserted that the *Norms* would "undermine human rights, the business sector of society, and the right to development" by "privatizing human rights" and inappropriately shifting state responsibilities to companies.

At that point I wasn't yet working for John Ruggie. I had just moved into the policy team at BP as my new colleagues were drafting BP's response to the commission's call for public input on the *Norms*. My colleagues wanted to make sure there was some business input that was more constructive than that of the chamber, but had plenty of concerns.

We wrote that a "set of Norms that lay out code of conduct–like responsibilities and expectations of businesses with regard to human rights, based on the Universal Declaration of Human Rights, constructed through a multi-stakeholder engagement process and agreed by governments is something that BP can support." But we also wrote that the "tone" of the

Norms ignored the positive contribution that business can have to human rights; that business "cannot and should not be held accountable for" government duties; and that the *Norms*' "proposed monitoring and verification process is vaguely defined and impractical."

BP was practically alone as a company expressing even tepid support for the *Norms*. Business opposition was likely due to more than content: the *Norms* were drafted by a five-man working group: one U.S. academic, a Senegalese judge, and diplomats from Korea, Cuba, and Russia. There were no business representatives on the working group, nor was there substantive consultation with the corporate community until late in the drafting process.

With businesses lining up against the *Norms*, governments felt like they had to drop the initiative even while some NGOs like Amnesty International expressed their support, saying that the *Norms* should "be used as the main basis to enable companies to fulfil their responsibilities in relation to human rights." In 2004 the Commission on Human Rights declined to consider the *Norms*, saying they "contain useful elements and ideas for consideration" but had "no legal standing."

Even with the *Norms* officially set aside, the question of what responsibilities business had for human rights remained. The Commission on Human Rights passed a resolution recommending to U.N. Secretary-General Kofi Annan that he appoint an independent expert to "identify and clarify" corporate responsibility for human rights, with further instruction about elaborating the role of government in regulating business with respect to human rights; clarifying concepts like "complicity" and "sphere of influence"; and developing materials and best practices.

Annan turned to John Ruggie, who had served as assistant

secretary-general earlier in his term and since returned to academia at the Harvard Kennedy School. John jokes that he was heavily sedated and recovering from hip replacement surgery when he took the call from Annan or else he never would have accepted the assignment, since what began as a part-time two-year post became an all-consuming six-year odyssey. His official title was "Special Representative of the Secretary-General on the issue of human rights and transnational corporations and other business enterprises," though he was generally referred to by the much less unwieldy "Special Representative on business and human rights."

Most U.N. appointees limit these unfunded assignments to doing a few official country visits and coming to Geneva once a year to present a report. But as John embarked on his mandate he realized its scope and complexity in terms of both politics and content—and the opportunity to have a positive impact. He began holding one-on-one meetings with those who had been involved in the *Norms* debate to understand their views without the posturing of public meetings. When he first came to BP to hear how we managed human rights, he impressed me as he asked good questions, played back what he had heard, and shared observations from other meetings.

I found John just as skilled in public venues. In the first consultation I attended, he didn't say much over the course of the day apart from an occasional clarifying question, no matter how contentious the proceedings became. But his day-end summary managed to incorporate a bit of each stakeholder's perspective, so everyone felt listened to. John partnered with the Business and Human Rights Resource Centre, a London-based nonprofit web portal, to devote a section of its website to not just his reports and speeches but any correspondence or material anyone submitted to him, so their input would have a public platform as well as informing John's mandate. The more that people felt like they were contributing to the mandate, the more that others wanted to join the party.

John's team became reflective of the array of stakeholders involved in his mandate. I created a position for BP to support my working with him beginning in 2006; diplomats from the United Kingdom and Switzerland did the same with the support of their governments; an NGO seconded one of its staff; and John raised funds from governments to hire international lawyers and policy analysts.

Beyond his little motley crew of a team, John became a Pied Piper of a much larger virtual community. NGOs organized meetings for him, companies road tested his ideas, academics contributed research, and interested parties submitted commentary and showed up to our consultations. I drafted discussion papers that we posted on our website to invite public comment on topics such as human rights impact assessments, like the study I had commissioned for BP in Indonesia; organized consultations and site visits, like the Coca-Cola visit to Colombia and a meeting on human rights and finance that included representatives from banks and export credit agencies from around the world. I participated on John's behalf in the Business Leaders Initiative on Human Rights, a small group of companies wanting to show leadership on human rights similar to the Business Leaders Initiative on Climate Change; and the Global Network Initiative, the effort by Microsoft, Google, and Yahoo! to work with human rights groups and other experts to develop a voluntary code of conduct to protect free expression and privacy. It was hard to find an industry or issue that didn't have some relevance to the mandate.

Protect, Respect and Remedy

In 2007, as John's term was supposed to end, he requested and received a one-year extension from the Commission on Human Rights to move past the research he had done and develop recommendations. As his third year drew to a close (during which the Commission transitioned into the Human Rights Council), John decided that what the debate needed was a basic set of foundational principles, not a laundry list of recommendations. In his 2008 report to the Human Rights Council, John presented what he called a "conceptual framework," with the title of "Protect, Respect and Remedy"—much better than the previous *Norms on the Responsibilities of Transnational Corporations and Other Business Enterprises with Regard to Human Rights.*

The "Protect" section was aimed at states, spelling out their duty to protect people in their jurisdictions against human rights abuses by corporations. That governments have a duty to protect was not new; but one common complaint from companies operating in developing countries was that governments seemed to be shirking their responsibilities. As I saw with BP in Indonesia, companies end up taking on tasks that should be done by government, like building schools, roads, and hospitals. Campaigners had similar concerns about governments' absence, but for different reasons: not only were states failing to do good things, they were failing to prevent companies from doing bad things. Governments hungry for investment didn't want to burden businesses with regulation or punish violations of local law, due to lack of will or capacity. So the "Protect" section of the framework was about governments fulfilling the duties that they already had as members of the United Nations.

The "Respect" section was aimed at companies. The failed

Norms had tried to impose on companies all of the same duties for human rights that governments have—in U.N.-speak, to promote, fulfill, respect, and protect. The business lobby thought this was too broad and inappropriate, and John agreed. In his 2006 report to the Human Rights Council he wrote: "While it may be useful to think of corporations as 'organs of society,' in the preambular language of the Universal Declaration, they are specialized organs, performing specialized functions. They are not a microcosm of the entire social body. By their very nature, therefore, corporations do not have a general role in relation to human rights like states, but a specialized one."

While some companies engage in philanthropy, build infrastructure, and do other good deeds, John wanted to set a minimum global standard, which he articulated as "respect." In other words, companies should adopt a human rights policy and conduct due diligence on human rights, as they do on so many other topics, to "know and show" that no infringements of human rights are occurring. Human rights due diligence should include assessing actual and potential human rights impacts on an ongoing basis; integrating the findings from those assessments across company operations; and tracking and reporting performance.

Some parties on opposite ends of the ideological spectrum thought "respect" didn't go far enough. A few multinational companies who invested heavily in responsible supply chain practices and community relations, like those in the Business Leaders Initiative on Human Rights, wanted every other company to have to do the same, while some campaigners wanted higher mandatory requirements for business. But John said that his aim was to set a universal standard to which all companies could be held.

The third pillar of John's framework, "Remedy," was about making sure that victims of corporate-related abuse had access to justice. Every company should make available some sort of mechanism, similar to a customer service or worker hotline, for stakeholders to air human rights issues before they escalate into serious problems and violence. Such mechanisms would save money and prevent harm, but should not preclude other avenues like the court system and other governmental and quasi-governmental entities.

To illustrate the "Remedy" pillar, John often spoke about his 2006 visit to the Yanacocha mine in Peru run by Newmont, a U.S. mining company. The surrounding community routinely blocked the access road to the mine out of anger over a myriad of issues including inadequate compensation for resettlement, lack of job opportunities, and environmental damage. In 2004, thousands of people descended to protest a proposed expansion of the mine, clashing with police; the expansion was postponed. John asked one of the community leaders why they resorted to such extreme measures instead of peacefully approaching the company. He replied: "They don't listen to us when we come with small problems, so we have to create big ones." A grievance mechanism to handle those small problems might have headed off the protests, saved Newmont a lot of time, money, and trouble, and prevented harm to the company's long-term neighbors.

The "Protect, Respect and Remedy" framework was welcomed by the Human Rights Council. The council was supportive of not only what he had produced but how he had done so, citing his "comprehensive, transparent and inclusive consultations conducted with relevant and interested actors in all regions." The council gave him another three-year mandate to "operationalize" the framework by developing "practical" and "concrete" guidance for states, businesses, and other stakeholders.

John jokes that no good deed goes unpunished, as he was given three more years to continue working around the clock and around the world for no pay. But he had already managed to achieve what seemed unthinkable a few years earlier: consensus among a wide range of previously opposed parties on some fundamental concepts.

How did he find consensus out of so much contention? Consultation and partnership were operating principles of John's mandate from the beginning, in part because he had limited money and manpower to conduct research and hold meetings.

He also had strategic and political motivations for doing so much outreach. No matter how enthusiastically his recommendations were eventually endorsed by the Human Rights Council, they were still just recommendations to a U.N. body, which had little control over or engagement with the primary actors in the issues he was addressing. As he later wrote in his book about his mandate, *Just Business*: "Students of international law and regulatory policy have long maintained that the perceived legitimacy of a rule-making process by those to whom the rules apply exerts a 'compliance pull,' increasing the chances that they will adhere to the rules." The more John reflected the view of companies as well as other societal actors, the more normative force his recommendations would have.

As he hoped, a wide variety of organizations started using the "Protect, Respect and Remedy" framework in their work, implicitly and explicitly. Two Australian senators passed a motion in 2008 calling on their government to implement the framework. In 2009 the U.K. Foreign and Commonwealth Office developed a *Business and Human Rights Toolkit* "to assist the staff of overseas missions by explaining how business operations may affect human rights." A campaign for divestment from Burma asserted that "The corporate responsibility to respect human rights is becoming the international norm." A South African think tank wrote in a submission to its parliament that John's 2008 report "emphasizes the state's duty to protect individual rights against abuse by non-state actors... It is this duty that we seek to urge MPs to take seriously in adopting the law reform proposals we recommend. Reform of corporate law represents one area where the state can fulfill its duty to protect." The National Business Association of Colombia passed a resolution in 2010 stating its commitment to promote the framework with its membership.

There was still far more work to do. After all, the "Protect, Respect and Remedy" framework was, as John explained in presenting it to the council, "a foundation on which thinking and action can build in a cumulative fashion." It did not contain specific instructions for what companies, governments, or civil society organizations must do. Some people found the notion of a framework difficult to grasp. The editor of a journal to which I submitted an article about John's mandate asked whether the framework was meant to replace the Universal Declaration on Human Rights. (No.) My husband half-joked, "It took you guys three years to come up with three words?" (Yes.)

But so far, John had succeeded in creating agreement and ownership of that foundation among the range of parties that would have to live with its implications, which was a significant achievement.

Distributing Ownership

Other Corporate Idealists know that their success lies in getting others to become champions of their work. Rona Starr, who runs the Supplier Workplace Accountability (SWA) program at

McDonald's, told me about a time when a senior executive in an unrelated function mentioned SWA before she did—and she was thrilled. "Every time I raise my hand people go, 'Oh crap, SWA, here we go.' It really gets legs when other people start to talk about it, not just me." Charlotte Grezo, who has worked in sustainability roles in a range of industries, told me that one of her personal key performance indicators is "when senior people think it was all their own idea, then that's got to be good."

As Dave Stangis, vice president of public affairs and corporate responsibility for Campbell's Soup, told me, "The levers have to be theirs, not mine." When he first came to the company in 2008, then-CEO Doug Conant was keen to emulate the simplicity and boldness of the sustainability goals that Lee Scott announced for Walmart in 2005—and he wanted to do it quickly. "He said, 'We can do this right now. Let's walk down the hall, meet with our [senior vice president] of the supply chain network, and we'll do this in ten minutes.' I said, 'We can do this in five minutes, you and I, but I want to do this collaboratively. Let me get the business and functional leaders to set the goals and agree on the framework. They will be more invested and the strategy will have staying power.'" Doug Conant agreed to Dave's approach, which ended up with such distributed ownership of the sustainability goals (such as reducing energy and water use and waste) that they're factored into incentive compensation for managers and senior executives across the company.

Creating ownership is an important skill in all sectors. Arvind Ganesan, director of Human Rights Watch's Business and Human Rights Division, told me: "The one-sentence description of advocacy that I think is best is: 'Good advocacy is getting somebody to think that it is in their interest to do what you want them to do.' The only way you can effectively do that is if you understand where other people are coming from."

As best-selling author and entrepreneurship guru Seth Godin has written, "If it's about your mission, about spreading the faith, about seeing something happen, not only do you not care about credit, you actually *want* other people to take credit."

Bureaucracy and Confusion

There were comfortingly familiar echoes of Corporate Idealist stories and experiences in the U.N. work and it was obviously going well, given the Human Rights Council's extension of John Ruggie's mandate and the diverse global community of people and organizations actively involved. But as the novelty of being free from BP wore off, I realized that the U.N. world was not for me. There was no orientation when I started working with John, so much of the U.N. semantics, protocols, and politics flew over my head. We were working virtually, with John in Boston, me in New York, and other team members in Geneva, Melbourne, and Bologna, which made formal communication tough and informal processing even tougher. The daily deluge of reply-all e-mails drowned out my nonurgent questions about particular decisions or procedures.

Of course there were politics and jargon at BP, but I had been at the company for long enough that I generally felt as though I knew what was going on. After all, everyone in the company was there to produce energy and bring it to market. Obviously there was complexity and debate over how to do that—for example, some of us were focused on minimizing disruption to communities and the environment as we pursued our mission—but for the most part I found everyone aligned toward a common goal.

In contrast, everyone seemed to have a different idea about

what John should be doing with his U.N. mandate. Communities living near controversial company operations thought he should be investigating their specific situations; human rights campaigners thought he should be drafting new international laws; companies thought he should be clarifying what they *don't* have to do; governments thought he should be informing and consulting them but certainly not telling them what regulations to enact. John made various attempts to convey his view of his mandate through speeches, articles, and constant conversation over e-mail and in person, but that didn't seem to sway others from their views.

The confusion that I felt about the mandate's purpose was exacerbated by the U.N. bureaucracy, which at times crossed the line from frustrating to ridiculous. One year we had trouble planning John's trip to present at the Human Rights Council because the Office of the High Commissioner for Human Rights, which organizes the council meetings, was debating whether to have the slate of independent experts present in alphabetical order by their last name or their topic. Luckily "Ruggie" and "transnational corporations" were close enough alphabetically that we were able to figure out what week to send him to Geneva, but I was astonished at the amount of time spent on the question. The eventual solution was to tag each mandate to one of the thirty articles in the Universal Declaration of Human Rights and, according to an e-mail I saw, "the order of consideration of reports follows the articles of the UDHR and than [sic] within an article it is by alphabetical order." However, the schedule didn't make clear what article John's mandate was associated with, and I was never able to find out.

In some respects I came to appreciate the bureaucracy and understand its purpose. The first time I attended a U.N. session, I was stunned by how the "interactive dialogue" was anything but. Participants read prepared statements while a huge screen at the front of the room counted down their allotted time to speak: ten minutes for each panelist with two additional minutes for each country visit they had done; then a two-minute right of reply from the country visited; then a two-minute right of reply for any country mentioned in the first country's statement; then two-minute comments and questions from the floor, which might or might not be addressed in the ten minutes the panelists were given to respond to all (or none) of the questions they received. The chairman pounded his gavel when the clock hit 00:00, which sometimes silenced the speaker but often didn't.

The acoustics in the hall were so bad that to hear the proceedings one had to put on the earpiece that was attached to each seat, where one could choose simultaneous translation into any of the six official U.N. languages. (I tried not to think about how many ears had been in the earpiece before mine.) Since anyone interested in the topic being presented had an earpiece on, the rest of the audience chatted with one another, e-mailed and surfed on the guest Wi-Fi network, and ate their lunch. During the questions and answers everyone would listen to the opening of a question to hear if it was directed at the speaker they were most interested in, and if not go back to their side conversations. Apparently the real work took place in the conversations along the back of the room and in the building's café.

At first this seemed to me like a ludicrous waste of time. But for many small countries and organizations this was their one and only opportunity to have a voice on a global stage, even if no one seemed to be reacting in real time. The extensive rules were needed to enforce equity: on what other platform do tiny nations like Suriname and the Maldives have the same two minutes to speak as the mighty United States?

On that level, I got it. The prepared statements are

negotiated and communicated ahead of time, read for the record, and the implications of those statements are similarly hashed out afterwards. But when John e-mailed to our team a satirical 2009 video by *The Onion* detailing the forcible take-over of the U.N. by a power-hungry Ugandan ambassador, it was less hilarious in its absurdity than sad in its familiarity: the on-site anchor describing the terrifying scene said that the new despotic leader "has the ability to do anything, from outline the U.N.'s year-long goals to propose agenda items for consider-ation by the Security Council... There's no telling what a mad-man like Mtambi will do!"

Building Relationships and Respect

While the U.N. bureaucracy was getting me down, my spirits were kept up by getting to know people from all corners of the world and walks of life, and watching what happened when such diverse characters got together. Often the most meaning-ful episodes happened in the evening hours after our formal consultations, when everyone was done stating their institu-tional positions.

One frigid night after a consultation in Berlin in January 2010, I ventured out in search of dinner with a small random group of participants. Among us were two people whose orga-nizations were ostensibly on opposite sides of the debate over international human rights standards for corporations: Adam Greene, head of labor relations and corporate social responsibil-ity for the U.S. Council for International Business, the Ameri-can arm of the International Chamber of Commerce, which had been staunchly opposed to the draft *Norms*; and Chris Joch-nick, head of the Private Sector team for Oxfam America and a passionate advocate for strengthening corporate legal accountability. We huddled together as we wandered lost through the streets, found the glowing light of a traditional beer hall, and warmed up over copious amounts of German beer and pork. Eventually we all found ourselves on the dance floor of the restaurant, having scared off the ballroom dance class that had been taking place while we ate. Adam pulled out his rusty 1980s break-dancing moves, with Chris cheering him on.

Back in the conference hall the next day, those of us who'd been out the night before winked at each other through our hangovers. Everyone went back to their institutional positions, but I had gained greater respect for Adam and Chris—not for their partying skills (as admirable as they were), but for the fact that they were fun, good-hearted people whose passion for their work was professional and sincere. And I could see that we were all aligned in wanting to see greater respect for human rights in business, even if we disagreed on how to get there.

Other Corporate Idealists told me that getting to know people outside of work proved crucial to moving beyond knee-jerk antagonism to respectful debate. Anna Murray of Young Women in Energy had to travel to remote mining operations in her previous role as manager of stakeholder engagement for GlencoreXstrata. She told me that "playing darts and having beers with the guys after work" unquestionably helped her work: "Relationship building happens outside the office. Half of it for me is building the network. The other half of it is being at the table, having value-add ideas, and baring your teeth early on to show that you're not a pushover."

One advocate drew a similar distinction, that the purpose of building relationships was not to smooth over differences but to engage with them properly—if relationships should be built at all. Mila Rosenthal led the business work for Amnesty

International USA, among the many human rights roles that she's held in her career:

> Yes, it's a fundamental truth that relationships do help in the same way that they help inside companies. But I worry about there being something a little corrupt about that too. It might be good to be rude when somebody's polluting your backyard and destroying your kids' health and taking the roof from over your head. If someone is dying with the factory ceiling falling down then they shouldn't be polite. You are speaking truth to power.
>
> It's certainly a fear that you carry around when you're coming from [the human rights NGO] perspective, the fear that you will be co-opted, that they will quote you as someone they've engaged with, that they will use it as cover for whatever they're doing. That they'll say, "Oh yes, I'm friends with Mila from Amnesty, we had a beer together in Geneva and she really understands where we're coming from with this, of course Amnesty can't say it publicly."
>
> This is not even particular to businesses because it's the same with governments—that is where people are being tortured and arrested and are suffering, you don't necessarily want to be chummy with the people who are making it happen.

Nostalgia Upended

I appreciated the U.N. work and the people taking part in it, but I was starting to feel nostalgic about corporate life. At the U.N. meetings, I found myself drifting toward the company representatives during our coffee breaks, eager to hear their latest stories from the field, nodding empathetically when they talked about their internal battles with their managers and in-house lawyers.

Then, on April 20, 2010, the Deepwater Horizon rig exploded in the Gulf of Mexico, killing eleven workers and wreaking environmental and economic havoc across the gulf and beyond. Subsequent news stories and congressional hearings painted a picture of BP as "taking too many risks and cutting corners in pursuit of growth and profits"—President Obama even chided the company's "recklessness" in a prime-time Oval Office address.

I began to question everything I thought I knew about business and what I had done in the previous ten years. If a company that I believed was doing the right thing on human rights and the environment could have done so much wrong, could I really contribute to the U.N. work—or for that matter, to the broader cause of responsible business? It seemed a joke for me to claim expertise in corporate responsibility with BP dominating my résumé, although I would later realize that experience in a company where things have gone wrong is more valuable than being around when everything has run smoothly. But at the time I wondered: Had I learned anything at all?

Fielding Criticism

On January 11, 2011, John Ruggie delivered a lecture at the Royal Society of Arts in London. With five months left to his mandate and the draft Guiding Principles newly out for public comment, he delivered a comprehensive narrative about the history leading up to his assignment, the process he had undertaken so far, and his hopes for the next phase.

His speech was covered favorably in the *Financial Times*, no small triumph for a story that didn't have a timely news hook or feature a prominent brand. John was careful not to name countries or companies in public statements, not knowing who might have connections to a Human Rights Council delegate who could jeopardize the political success of his mandate. This avoidance of specificity was savvy from the U.N. perspective but made it hard to attract the attention of mainstream media. For example, in the run-up to the 2008 Beijing Olympics, John fielded calls from reporters trying to get him to say something bad about China's human rights record or how certain Olympic sponsors should use their leverage with the government; his refusal to do so contributed to China's vocal support of his work and the ongoing engagement of those corporate sponsors.

Five days after the first *Financial Times* article, the same journalist found a more intriguing angle. "Rights groups slam U.N. plan for multinationals," read the headline. The article cited a "strongly-worded statement" by Amnesty International, Human Rights Watch, and five other human rights groups that John's proposals "risk undermining efforts to strengthen corporate responsibility and accountability for human rights." Specifically, the groups wanted more explicit instruction to states on how to regulate companies and to companies on what they must and must not do.

It was inevitable that human rights campaigners would want higher standards; groups whose mission is to protect the world's most vulnerable people rarely claim victory. But John fired off a letter to the editor that called their criticism of the draft Guiding Principles "bizarre," and said they "would have a lot to answer for if they actually were to oppose Human Rights Council endorsement of this hard-won initiative," as they would be "delivering 'nothing' to victims yet again."

Arvind Ganesan of Human Rights Watch wrote back to the *Financial Times* that it is "unfortunate that Prof. Ruggie would claim that human rights organisations that do not endorse his views are a greater threat to local communities than unregulated businesses and governments that may actually commit abuses against them."

John came back again: "While AI [Amnesty International] and others have been busy writing letters justifying their indefensible advice to the U.N. Human Rights Council, Amnesty U.K. has been busy 'urging' the UK House of Commons select committee on business, innovation and skills to adopt the very proposals that Amnesty's international secretariat finds so inadequate... One is tempted merely to say, 'Amnesty, meet Amnesty.'"

The exchange seemed to me to echo the antagonism that had characterized the *Norms* debate years earlier. However, I didn't appreciate at the time that there was a tactical reason for John's behavior. He had to come out swinging to show the Human Rights Council a counterpoint to the NGOs' argument before any council delegates took their concerns as truth. "I didn't do many of these things by accident," he later told me. "I usually had a reason, I wasn't just blowing off steam." He paused. "Usually," he smiled. He admitted that the *Financial Times* letters might have been "intemperate," but was adamant about following the philosophy of President Bill Clinton's handlers, to never miss a news cycle.

At the same time, his standing up to NGOs potentially strengthened his support among businesses. Not that John had fielded any serious criticism from the business community, at least not for a while. Three years earlier, in 2008, John woke up to a memo in his inbox written by Martin Lipton, a well-known American lawyer and corporate governance expert. The memo warned that the "Protect, Respect and Remedy" framework "could impose on businesses an array of expansive obligations that require close attention by corporate management and boards." Lipton also suggested that the framework could "impose on corporations the obligation to compensate for the political, civil, economic, social, or other deficiencies of the countries in which they conduct business."

Seeing an influential voice like Lipton come out against the framework a few weeks before the Human Rights Council would vote on it had John worried. "My heart fell into my stomach," he later told me. "I didn't think a response by me would be adequate, because who am I? I had no credibility in the corporate law community." John reached out to Ira Milstein, an equally respected corporate governance and law expert, who wrote a counter memo: "Rather than being alarmed, U.S. corporations should welcome the Special Representative's proposals as a means to facilitate leveling of the international corporate playing field by bringing foreign firms in line with U.S. standards for respect of human rights."

For John it wasn't enough to rebut Lipton's criticism—he wanted to win him over. John invited Lipton to one of our expert meetings on corporate law, which he eagerly attended, and consulted with him as our research on corporate law and human rights evolved. Sure enough, when John put out a draft of his final recommendations in 2011, Lipton wrote: "This draft report's sensible guidance will be widely applauded. 'Guiding Principles' insightfully marries aspirations with practicality... The draft report's eminently reasonable guiding principles can be endorsed, and practically implemented, by corporations."

John had worked so hard to engage with companies in the first few years of his mandate, and convey that he was interested in what would mitigate their risks and achieve greater consistency in what was expected of them, that they had stayed fairly quiet. Adam Greene of the U.S. Council for International Business invoked the movie *Jerry Maguire* in telling me his organization's feelings towards John: "He had us at 'hello.'" The core of John's recommendations for business was to conduct human rights due diligence, which was language that sounded perfectly reasonable to business. For any company to implement John's recommendations to the letter would actually take a great deal of effort, but no one could object on principle.

As John's concerns over company opposition faded, so did the importance of my role as his liaison to the business community. John assigned me to reach out to companies that had been involved in the mandate to see if they would be willing to publicly endorse the Guiding Principles to demonstrate business support leading up to the final council meeting. We got statements from GE Cerrejón Coal in Colombia, Sakhalin Energy in Russia, and others, which we posted on our website.

I was ready to move on—but to what? I still believed the U.N. work was important, but lost focus every time our team had another debate on whether it would be better for the Human Rights Council to "welcome" or "endorse" John's final recommendations. At the time I understood that the council had never applied "endorse" to a text that they didn't themselves negotiate, but I did not understand the importance of that fact, which John later explained to me:

The last year, a lot of my thinking was concerned with what kind of verb we could get out of the Human Rights Council. You can't get anything more out of the U.N. human rights machinery [than "endorse"]. I wanted to get as much as possible so that there would be as robust a foundation as possible.

I made two assumptions: one was that people who weren't crazy about what we were doing would, at that point, throw in the towel and say, "Okay, this is what we've got to work with for now. We're not going to get anything else out of the Human Rights Council that is going to top this. So let's stop fighting it for a while and work with this."

Secondly, starting as far back as 2008, I realized that whatever came out of the Human Rights Council in and of itself wasn't going to be enough, that we would have to sell this to other entities. "Endorse" just made that a lot easier.

The public and private dialogue, the research, the language—all of these elements had to work individually and together if a U.N. report was to have real-world impact.

During the first half of 2011 the members of our team with U.N. experience and contacts were in high gear, reaching out to delegates and serving as John's representatives. From their outreach and from the online consultation I managed on the draft Guiding Principles that gathered more than thirty-five hundred comments from around the world, we were receiving a lot of positive feedback. We were cautiously optimistic that the Guiding Principles would win endorsement.

Even so, the Deepwater Horizon disaster shook my faith in the power of documents like the Guiding Principles. I had poured a lot of energy into developing the human rights guidance note at BP, which was one of many tools that were supposed to govern behavior, along with a code of conduct and numerous safety policies. Enron had a Code of Ethics that included all of the right words about ethics and integrity. But none of those measures prevented the problems at both companies. Did these pieces of paper—policies, codes, principles, declarations—make any difference?

At the time I wasn't sure. In the meantime, I was pretty sure a U.N. career was not in my future. Nor did I see myself as one of the advocates I had gotten to know. Just as I didn't appreciate the tactics of John's *Financial Times* letters, I didn't fully grasp that what I thought was impracticality on the part of human rights NGOs was also strategic. As Arvind Ganesan of Human Rights Watch told me later: "You need NGOs pushing the envelope far beyond where the U.N. or the companies or governments are willing to go, because that is what creates the firmament and the environment to start doing something." Those tactics didn't resonate with me; I had always been inclined to seek common ground right off the bat.

I saw the importance of all of these different stakeholder roles, but in my confusion I couldn't figure out if any of them were right for me. As John's mandate barreled toward its close, I had plenty else to occupy my energy: my husband and I were looking to buy a home in New York and start a family. Unsure which direction to lean in professionally, I ended up leaning back for a while.

The End of the Beginning

Despite my increasing detachment, as we all convened in Geneva for the June 2011 Human Rights Council session at which the council would vote on the Guiding Principles, I found myself as nervous as the rest of the team.

On the agenda that day was the usual array of unrelated topics: the resolution endorsing the Guiding Principles was slated after a resolution on the right to education and before one on extrajudicial, summary, and arbitrary executions. The audience seemed typically distracted, but for Team Ruggie, as we had come to refer to ourselves, tension filled the room and all eyes were on John.

As the team's self-appointed social media guru, I channeled my energy into Twitter, relaying delegations' remarks on the Guiding Principles as they were delivered and fielding good wishes from those around the world watching the livestream on the U.N. website.

As predicted, Norway and Argentina spoke first as two of the five sponsors of the resolution endorsing the Guiding Principles. (The three other sponsors were India, Nigeria, and Russia, so the resolution had one sponsor from each U.N. regional group.) The United States spoke next: Daniel Baer, deputy assistant secretary of state for Democracy, Human Rights and Labor, said that the U.S. "would like to thank and congratulate the special representative for the important progress he has made on this challenging issue, and express our support and commitment to working to make the vision of the Guiding Principles a reality where it matters most—on the ground for people and businesses."

Ecuador sounded the one note of concern, that "the resolution swept aside several issues important for setting up a binding legal framework," but said that "it would not stand in the way of consensus out of consideration of the five sponsoring countries." Hungary, the United Kingdom, and Japan all delivered remarks expressing their support for the resolution, then the Office of the High Commissioner for Human Rights delivered a *pro forma* summary of the cost implications of the resolution's proposal to set up a five-person working group to "promote the effective and comprehensive dissemination and implementation of the Guiding Principles" and convene an annual multistakeholder forum.

Finally, there was no one left in the queue to speak. The chairman banged his gavel and announced that the resolution would pass without a vote. This was the outcome John had hoped for, which essentially meant unanimous support, avoiding a vote that would force any delegations with reservations to take an opposing stance.

I turned to look at John in the row behind me. His wife of forty-plus years had come along for this grand finale and was gripping his arm; his face was bright red and tears filled his eyes. Delegates and observers from around the room approached to congratulate him. I sent out one more tweet ("PASSED!!! #Human Rights Council endorses #Ruggie Principles!"), then joined the high fives and hugs. The council had moved onto the next agenda item, but there was so much commotion in our corner of the room that the chairman banged his gavel and called for order. We exited the building into the afternoon Geneva sun and walked to a nearby café for drinks.

The next day we all went to Bologna for a weekend of eating and touring that our colleague based there had organized. It was a lovely way to end the mandate but I had already mentally moved on, not having felt like a vital part of this mission for months. I was thrilled for John—this was a major achievement for him, a serious piece of legacy work—and for the others on the team who had worked so hard to win council approval.

Despite the abundance of wine and prosciutto, I had mixed feelings about both our output and my role in it. Part of me agreed with the critics who pointed out that the Guiding Principles were not legally binding on anyone. Even the governments that endorsed the Guiding Principles did not have to abide by them, never mind the companies. The Human Rights Council might choose to turn the Guiding Principles into a treaty that could be ratified by individual states, then adopted and enforced however they each saw fit. That process could take decades—if it got started at all.

The Power of Normative Standards

Yet from my experience I had more belief in the power of normative standards than those who criticized the principles for their lack of legal standing: advocates who want international law, and conservative business lawyers who believe there is no such thing. Companies, like individuals, do not act based simply on what is legal and what is not. Laws are part of what shapes our day-to-day behavior, but so are our goals and resources and interests, what our peers are doing, and the principles we subscribe to, whether professional, religious, philosophical, or otherwise.

BP's behavior in Indonesia and China was in part shaped by laws in those countries and in the United Kingdom, but also by what our peer companies and business partners were doing, codes we had signed up for like the Voluntary Principles on Security and Human Rights, what we thought would be in the best interests of our operations and the surrounding communities, public opinion, and our executives' personal experiences and beliefs.

John Ruggie was of a similar mind-set in believing in a mix of measures. Some advocates had urged him to focus on developing a treaty. But John stressed that there was no one single document, tool, or entity that would solve the complex challenges that arise at the intersection of business and human rights, and that these challenges needed to be approached from multiple angles at once. He repeatedly pointed out that the Declaration on the Rights of Indigenous Peoples, which the U.N. General Assembly adopted in 2007, had been twenty-two years in the making—and was still a nonbinding declaration.

Not that such declarations weren't important. John firmly believed in the normative power of the U.N. His faith may have been because he had worked with Kofi Annan, a persuasive and charismatic leader if ever there was one. (Annan agreed to cochair an advisory group of eminent persons that John convened for his mandate, along with Mary Robinson, former President of Ireland and U.N. High Commissioner for Human Rights. When we convened the group in Salzburg in 2009 Annan was only able to join by phone, but he managed to address everyone in the room personally and graciously. I've never seen so many distinguished people beaming at a speakerphone.)

Even without the backing of hard law, statements and declarations can have an impact. For example, a number of Corporate Idealists who work with suppliers in China have told me how helpful they find the 2010 video clip of China's delegation to the Human Rights Council saying that "The Chinese government attaches importance to the corporate responsibility of enterprises.... We attach importance to the protection of workers' rights." As I had learned working in Shanghai, whether or not there is enforcement the mere fact of a government statement carries a great deal of weight in China.

Governments might not adopt the U.N.'s documents as written, but might craft their own policies, positions, and laws in ways that are consistent with what the U.N. put forward, which can be just as useful. For example, in 2013 the U.S. State Department issued reporting requirements for U.S. companies heading into the newly opened markets of Burma, requiring information about "due diligence policies and procedures (including those related to risk and impact assessments) that address operational impacts on human rights," referencing the Guiding Principles in a footnote.

Other important entities have incorporated tenets of the Guiding Principles in some form. The Organisation for Economic Cooperation and Development (OECD) updated its Guidelines for Multinational Enterprises in 2011, soon after the Guiding Principles were endorsed, and included a new human rights chapter. At the OECD Summit presenting the new Guidelines, U.S. Secretary of State Hillary Clinton referenced the Guiding Principles and John Ruggie specifically. In 2010 the International Standards Organization (ISO) issued a new Social Responsibility Guidance, ISO 26000, that includes a human rights chapter.

The International Finance Corporation (IFC), the division of the World Bank that works with the private sector, updated its Sustainability Framework to reference the Guiding Principles, meaning that the companies that receive IFC funding could be required to implement the Guiding Principles. The Equator Principles, a standard for private banks that currently has about eighty signatories, were updated in 2013 and now require human rights due diligence. The Business and Human Rights Resource Centre adds more examples of the Guiding Principles being implemented every week.

Seeing all of this uptake gave me hope that these pieces of paper might matter after all. However, as of August 2013 only 330 companies have human rights policies, at least that are known by the Business and Human Rights Resource Centre. About seven thousand companies are signatories to the U.N. Global Compact, the initiative John Ruggie helped create under Kofi Annan's U.N. tenure, which asks companies to uphold ten principles, including two on human rights. That's a lot of signatories for one initiative, but Walmart has more than one hundred thosuand suppliers.

Would the Guiding Principles make a difference to the sugar plantation *patron* or bottling plant manager in Colombia we visited in 2007? Yes, if pressure to comply comes from Coca-Cola, FEMSA, the Colombian government, and any other stakeholders they listen to. Those two men may never hear of the Guiding Principles, but they might end up complying with them anyway.

Outside the Bubble

During the development of the Guiding Principles it sometimes felt as though we were traveling around the world to meet the same people over and over. In 2010 I saw Ed Potter from Coca-Cola more often than I saw my mother, albeit with lots of different people around every time we met.

Chris Jochnick of Oxfam believes that it was appropriate for a relatively limited core group to have been deeply involved in creating the Guiding Principles. "That's the downside, that it can create a little bubble," he told me. "On the other hand, for what John was after that was the right group of people. This was a process of coming up with a set of principles that John could get a certain U.N. body to sign. If the objective had been to bring the most recalcitrant companies to the table, that would have looked very different. But in lawmaking it's a very political calculation. You're not there to socialize and bring people on. At that moment, you're just out to build a critical coalition."

Chris countered my concerns not just about the mandate,

but also about having involved a select group of colleagues in creating BP's human rights guidance note. With regard to both the BP human rights guidance note and the U.N. Guiding Principles, the businesspeople who needed them the most and could speak to the issues were those operating in difficult environments and hungry for guidance, not those who didn't yet know there was a problem.

For the Guiding Principles to become widely known and taken up, the next few years would need to see them reach a much broader audience. That is part of the task of the five-person working group that the Human Rights Council established to succeed John Ruggie's mandate. Margaret Jungk is one of its members, an American who created and led the Human Rights and Business Department at the Danish Institute for Human Rights. She told me that she is very familiar with that feeling of seeing the same small group of people repeatedly from when she did her PhD in humanitarian intervention in the early 1990s:

> For the longest time I could predict who would be at any conference with 90 percent accuracy because it was the usual group of academics and state experts and U.N. people that would show up for every conference. We all knew what the other person was going to say. We all had our well-rehearsed ideas. We'd put them out there and then we'd pack up and go home.
>
> The human rights and business field is still at that stage. The humanitarian intervention field branched out tremendously in the fifteen years after that; now it's a very popular topic and you can never predict who will turn up or what they'll have to say about it. I think human rights and business will get into that mainstream eventually, but we're right now still in early days.

Margaret cited the seminal 1962 book *Diffusion of Innovations* by American sociologist Everett Rogers, who described the bell curve of new ideas or technologies catching on among innovators, then early adopters, then the early majority, late majority, and laggards. She told me, "I don't think we've even hit the early majority part of the curve yet; we're still talking as a group of innovators." Everett Rogers wrote that an innovation needs to reach a critical mass within a particular time period or else it won't survive. Margaret agrees: "We've got a certain time pressure now to make sure that we start attracting those new audiences and to explain the relevance and the value of the Framework and the Guiding Principles so they don't die an early death." Hopefully the momentum that John Ruggie generated during his mandate will be sustained.

My most important takeaway from the five years that I worked with John—apart from the difference between "welcome" and "endorse"—is the importance of creating ownership, that process can matter even more than substance. As John said in his 2011 speech at the Royal Society of Arts in London, "No matter how good your ideas may be, the manner in which they are produced matters greatly."

Cleaning out my mandate files in late 2011, I came across a document that a few of us wrote just for John in 2008, sketching out what we thought principles for companies might look like. They're very similar to what the council finally endorsed three years later. But had we handed in what we first wrote then, they never would have won the widespread support that they eventually did. Everyone had to feel ownership over the final product. The drafters of the *Norms* learned that the hard way, and John learned from their mistakes, actively seeking and incorporating feedback.

Another Corporate Idealist, Suzanne Stormer, who heads corporate responsibility for Danish pharmaceutical company Novo Nordisk, agrees that proactive engagement is critical. She told me: "I've got the power, but what we've learned is you actually have to consult. You have to consult even if it's inconvenient and even if it's not popular. Because you might as well take the battles before you go public. It's much more dangerous to go out with these bold statements and then afterwards need to build the coalition to support it."

After John's mandate ended in June 2011, Team Ruggie went our separate ways. John resumed his full academic duties at Harvard and became a senior advisor to law firm Foley Hoag's corporate social responsibility practice (run by Gare Smith, the lawyer I worked with in Indonesia to do BP's human rights impact assessment). John also agreed to chair the new Institute for Human Rights and Business, as well as a nonprofit that Team Ruggie colleagues set up to work with governments, companies, and NGOs to implement the Guiding Principles. John's book about the mandate, *Just Business,* was published in March 2013 and sold out its first printing within months.

The mandate inspired a number of organizations and initiatives named with various permutations of "human rights" and "business," including the Institute for Human Rights and Business and the Global Business Initiative on Human Rights, both of which grew out of the Business Leaders Initiative on Human Rights. American University started an Initiative for Human Rights in Business in 2011 and New York University's Stern School of Business created a Center for Business and Human Rights in 2013. (One is reminded of the exchange from the Monty Python movie *Life of Brian*: "Are you the Judean People's Front?" "'Judean People's Front?!' We're the People's Front of Judea!")

Despite the cottage industry blooming around the assignment I had just completed, I had no full-time employment and was unsure where to go and what I had to offer, happily married but professionally alone and adrift. I would later realize that such crises of confidence are hardly unusual for the Corporate Idealist.

Chapter 5

GULF OF MEXICO: CORPORATE IDEALISM IN CRISIS

May 26, 2010—London: From across St. James's Square, I could see Bill in the entrance to BP's headquarters. He was always the chattiest of the company's security guards.

"Haven't seen you in a while!" he said in his Scottish lilt. "How long's it been now?"

"Two years," I said.

"You're in New York now, right? We could use you back here, you know," he smiled. "Help me fight off those Greenpeace climbers." He pointed his chin to the roof. One week earlier, Greenpeace activists had scaled the building and hung a "British Polluters" banner off the fifth-floor balcony. "Took 'em forty-seven seconds," Bill said.

"How is it in there?" I nodded into the building.

"Oh, you can imagine," he said. "I tell ya', I feel sorry for Tony…"

Bill was one of the few people in the world who felt

sympathy for Tony Hayward, then BP's CEO. One month earlier, the Deepwater Horizon rig had exploded, killing eleven men and spewing millions of barrels of oil into the Gulf of Mexico. BP had not yet been able to cap the well, and anger was swelling among affected communities, regulators, and the millions of people watching the leak in real time via BP's underwater webcam.

I shared the world's frustration at the company's failed attempts at containing the damage; part of me wished I had scaled the building with Greenpeace. But at the same time, the image of BP dominating the headlines—a "scathing portrait of cultural failure," in the words of the *New York Times*—did not resemble the BP I had been part of for nine years. It wasn't *my* BP.

I was at home in New York on April 22 when I pulled up the *New York Times* website to learn that a rig had exploded in the Gulf of Mexico two nights earlier. Even though I left BP in 2008, nine years at the company imprinted in me a predictable sequence of emotions after hearing about an accident: anxiety, over whether it was your company; then relief, if it isn't; then perhaps a fleeting, shameful moment of schadenfreude; then a wave of sadness and a whole lot of "There but for the grace of God go I."

This time the relief never came. BP had leased the Deepwater Horizon rig, and quickly became the corporate face of the disaster. Over the subsequent months, numerous investigations, hearings, trials, and reports painted a horrible picture of a company whose "managers had become deaf to risk and systematically gambled with safety at hundreds of facilities and with thousands of employees' lives," as one piece put it. I read the coverage wide-eyed and slack-jawed, as the company that I loved for its progressive position on human rights and the environment was being pilloried for its alleged negligence of both.

At the time I was working full time for the United Nations special representative on business and human rights, charged with developing principles to prevent and address human rights abuses linked to business. I was the company representative on the team, there to contribute my experience with a multinational that had demonstrated that it was possible to embed human rights in policies and practices. I did work to that effect on two of the company's biggest projects in two of the most difficult countries to do business in, then worked with staff around the world to do the same. Surely the company I did all of that for, that in my experience went above and beyond what any law required to protect people and planet, was a model for others to follow. Wasn't it?

Maybe not. ProPublica, the respected independent news organization, did a joint investigation with PBS *Frontline* into BP after the spill, reporting that "the company repeatedly cut corners, let alarm and safety systems languish and skipped essential maintenance that could have prevented a number of explosions and spills." The National Commission on the BP Deepwater Horizon Oil Spill and Offshore Drilling recounted numerous safety incidents in BP's operations, concluding that: "These incidents and subsequent analyses indicate that the company does not have consistent and reliable risk-management processes." The commission cited a U.K. investigation into problems at BP's Grangemouth refinery in Scotland: "BP Group policies set high expectations but these were not consistently achieved because of organisational and cultural reasons." When BP CEO Tony Hayward testified in front of Congress, Representative Henry Waxman reprimanded him: "There is a complete contradiction between BP's words and deeds."

My perception of BP was the opposite of what was being described. In Indonesia and China, I had all the resources and support I needed to devise innovative and reliable processes to manage risk and help BP realize its expectations and aspirations. But some of the investigations emphasized the lack of consistency across the company. According to one *New York Times* article the administrator for the U.S. Occupational and Health Safety Administration said, "Senior management told us they are very serious about safety, but we observed that they haven't translated their words into safe working procedures and practices, and they have difficulty applying the lessons learned from refinery to refinery or even from within refineries." Perhaps my BP wasn't the only BP after all.

I was back in London four weeks after the spill to update my former colleagues about the U.N. mandate, a trip that had been planned months earlier. I had asked if they wanted to postpone the session, but they confirmed that about a dozen people were still keen to attend. On one hand, human rights had never been more relevant: eleven people had had their most fundamental right—the right to life—violated in the disaster. On the other hand, an hour thinking about something other than the gulf could have been a welcome respite.

I was happy to see former colleagues, but had to tone down the joyous reunions given the silence across every floor. One friend told me that people had been breaking down and crying in the hallways from stress and exhaustion, but needless to say weren't seeking or receiving any sympathy since lives had been lost.

But at the same time, business was carrying on. After my human rights session—mostly my talking about the U.N., wanting to give my spent-looking colleagues a break—I met with a colleague working on BP's business in the Middle East. She was of course concerned about the spill but had a job to do that couldn't have been further from the Gulf of Mexico.

I realized that my crisis of confidence in my former company and the work I had done there was exacerbated by my now being on the outside, where most of my information came from the mass media. (I was tempted to reach out to colleagues to get the inside scoop, but figured they had better things to do so restrained myself to a few "thinking about you, no need to reply" e-mails.) Visiting BP reminded me what it's like in a company during a crisis. Of course there are staff who go into overdrive and work 24–7 on the issue, and there's a palpable tension in the building, particularly on the executive floors. But at the same time, business carries on in the rest of the world. I was based in BP headquarters when BP's Texas City refinery exploded in 2005, killing fifteen people, and when two other incidents caused no fatalities but were still major problems: the $1 billion Thunder Horse rig in the Gulf of Mexico started listing precariously in 2005 after Hurricane Dennis due to a valve that was installed backward, and a pipeline in Alaska corroded in 2006 and leaked more than two hundred thousand gallons of oil. Everyone in the building was somber, and company-wide examinations of policies and practices ensued, but most of us kept our heads down and carried on with our work. The incidents didn't feel as wholly destabilizing to me back then as I assumed the Deepwater Horizon disaster was from my new outsider perch. As a Goldman Sachs spokesman said upon the release of a book about the bank by a former employee: "It's not unusual for a person to think the place he or she worked isn't the same after he has left."

Even so, I had been in a role that was supposed to help shape BP's practices and culture, and naïvely thought I had made progress toward a company in which everyone respected human rights. Was everything I thought I had learned about business wrong? Was my nine-year love affair with BP a sham?

It would take a few years of reflection and speaking with many other Corporate Idealists to decide.

Crises are Common

I am certainly not the only Corporate Idealist whose company has been linked to harm. On April 24, 2013, the Rana Plaza building in Bangladesh collapsed, killing more than eleven hundred garment workers. The disaster sparked consumer protests in front of Gap stores in the United States, Primark stores in the United Kingdom, and criticism of the many other Western brands that sourced in Bangladesh, whether or not they were found to have sourced at Rana Plaza specifically. The U.S. government suspended trade privileges with Bangladesh, and under pressure more than one hundred retailers signed on to new initiatives to upgrade factory safety.

Many of the brands whose goods were made in Rana Plaza had social compliance programs; at least two of the factories in Rana Plaza passed audits in the month before the collapse. But such audits generally focus on wages and working conditions, not the structural integrity of the buildings—even though the latter is known to be a serious problem in Bangladesh. Marcus Chung, who has worked in corporate responsibility for multiple companies, has blogged about the common practice of building factories on top of others, even on buildings zoned for residential use, since factories are rewarded with tax incentives and almost never visited by government inspectors. Sean Ansett, who has worked for Gap Inc., Apple, and Burberry told me, "The fact is that people are being disingenuous if they say they didn't know about the problems in Bangladesh. We've had numerous fires and collapses now for six years."

Knowing about a problem is one thing; assigning responsibility and taking action are another. If a Western brand is one of ten buyers from a supplier that occupies one-fifth of a floor in a building with ten floors and ten times as many companies, that Western brand is unlikely to take responsibility for the building's walls and foundations. The Bangladeshi government is supposed to update and enforce building and labor codes, but has little capacity (only eighteen labor inspectors for some one hundred thousand factories in the Dhaka district alone) and even less motivation (10 percent of the country's legislators own garment factories).

In retrospect, of course the brands should have included structural integrity in their audits, particularly in a country where that is known to be such a big risk. In fact, so many corporate disasters might have been predictable. In 2010, thirteen employees of Foxconn Technology Group committed suicide. The extensive global media coverage of the deaths sparked international shock and outrage, but not from Jeremy Prepscius, who worked for Nike in Vietnam and now oversees Asia for BSR (formerly Business for Social Responsibility): "Suicide in factories—really, it's a surprise? Anybody with people on the ground working on these issues for any time in China realizes we have eighteen- to twenty-four-year-olds for the very first time leaving home, in a difficult work environment, living in a dormitory with six other people in their room. Uh, challenges? Yeah."

Scanning for potential disasters ahead of time should certainly be the purview of a company's CEO, of the board of directors—and an even larger part of the job of the Corporate Idealist. Some "corporate social responsibility" or "corporate citizenship" jobs are about organizing employee volunteer programs and charitable donations, but the Corporate Idealists I've gotten to know are grappling with the most difficult aspects of multinational business, challenges that are deeply embedded in their industries: sourcing of apparel and footwear in countries with poor infrastructure and few protections for workers, creation of technology that can be used to disseminate ideas but also for surveillance, changing the lives of communities around extractive projects.

These businesses are inherently complex and inherently risky. But in many corporate disasters the risks are well-known, at least their general nature, if not their specifics. And as the Presidential Oil Spill Commission noted, "Even inherently risky businesses can be made safer, given the right motivations and systems-safety management practices."

If these disasters are foreseeable and preventable, why do they keep happening? From my conversations with Corporate Idealists a few themes emerged; these do not comprise a comprehensive analysis of capitalism's failings nor of any one disaster. But they do illustrate some of the challenges of preventing harm.

People Hide Bad News

One reason is that conditions on the ground can be tough to assess, whether because of the complexity of the context or deliberate obfuscation. Sean Ansett told me about bringing one of his former CEOs to India: "There were clear messages made to the suppliers that the CEO wants to see the factory as it is: it shouldn't be touched up, it should be as it typically runs. When the CEO landed, the first factory they went in, it was highly embarrassing for the team because you could smell the fresh paint on the walls—they obviously painted it recently." Ed Potter, director of global workplace rights for The Coca-Cola

Company, told me about one visit to a factory making branded products for his company: "Everybody had these perfectly pristine lab coats on, and perfectly pristine face masks. Under the pretense of going back because I had forgotten something I walked back in there and they were all turning in those lab coats and face masks."

Ed's and Sean's stories are common—and not new. In *The China Price: The True Cost of Chinese Competitive Advantage,* Alexandra Harney details the "epidemic of falsification" among Chinese factories—and cites a journalist's account of similar practices in American cotton mills in the early 1900s, when "even the children are taught to lie about their age, and their tongues are ever ready with the glib rehearsal. Some mills keep a look-out for the inspector, and at the danger signal the children scurry like rats to hide in attics, to crouch in cellars, behind bales of cotton, under heaps of old machinery." According to Harney, the only difference today is "scale and skill."

Factory owners will hide bad news if failing an audit means losing business. As one commentator wrote after U.K. beef supplies were found to contain horse meat: "Overstretched suppliers were dealing with demanding contract conditions in the only way they knew how. In the absence of a long-term commitment from their customer, they focused on a tactical fix to protect their small profit margins and keep themselves competitive enough to successfully win the next, short-term contract extension." Some companies like the Swedish clothing retailer H&M have stated their intent to extend contracts with suppliers to build deeper relationships through which they can address issues together and remove the incentives to lie. But such efforts can be undercut if the factory doesn't have the skills or capacity to meet changing demand or if macroeconomic shifts mean another country emerges as a more appealing place to source.

So factories do whatever it takes to win business. As Jeremy Prepscius of BSR told me, "There's always one good factory, and there's always one that lies better than everybody else. So guess which one would have the cheaper price?"

No matter how much effort might go into hiding bad news, saying that the world's best-resourced multinationals can get duped by small factory owners may be generous to the latter; it would be hard to avoid information about poor working conditions in China or Bangladesh.

The work of the Corporate Idealist is indeed not to avoid but to seek out those problems. Laura Rubbo, a senior leader in Disney's International Labor Standards program, told me about a trip she took to Istanbul in 2000 (before she joined Disney). She visited a small jewelry workshop that looked fine with respect to working conditions. But as she left the building she saw a small staircase leading downstairs and decided to follow it:

Without the people upstairs knowing what we did we walked into this basement where there were, I would guess, ten-, eleven-, twelve-year-old boys working in the dark shaping metal over open pits of fire, shirtless; I'm not even sure if they were wearing shoes. This metal was clearly going upstairs. The workshop upstairs looked fine, but here we had child labor, exposure to open flames, no time clock, and no fire extinguishers.

Part of me thought, "I wish I hadn't seen this," and part of me is glad I saw it. Because it opens your eyes and it teaches you that you always have to ask the next question. You always have to walk down the basement steps, and you always have to walk upstairs to the women's dorm, and you always have to walk through the dorm to walk into the bathroom. You have to be inquisitive and you can't accept on face value that this is the way the product was made. There are the finished product factories or the workshops, but what's happening behind the scenes?

Few People Bear Witness

Sadly, if an executive doesn't see problems firsthand, he or she is much less likely to commit resources to addressing them. As John Kotter of Harvard Business School writes in *The Heart of Change*: "People change what they do less because they are given *analysis* that shifts their *thinking* than because they are *shown* a truth that influences their *feelings*." Even the most numbers-driven executive can only be brought so far with an economic argument.

Laura Rubbo of Disney told me that her department has facilitated factory visits for the company's chief financial officer and other executives. Her team's aim was "to present senior management with an honest look into how the company's branded products were made—a view of the good, the bad, and the ugly." The visits were to randomly selected factories in keeping with their normal audit process. Laura said, "They saw well-performing factories, like one that participated in the Better Work Vietnam program [a partnership of the International Labour Organization and the International Finance Corporation]. But they also saw mediocre and even some poorly performing facilities that did not meet our standards for basic cleanliness and safety. I was glad that they saw a full range." That firsthand experience helped Laura's team continue to gain senior-level understanding and approval for their work.

Sean Ansett, formerly of Gap Inc., Apple, and Burberry, told me that when he hasn't been able to bring senior executives to see factories, photographs have worked:

> I remember one time presenting to the CEO and CFO and bringing in photographs of a factory in China, real photographs of a factory that we produced in, and people were appalled. In subsequent meetings there was proactive follow up by the CEO and CFO saying, "Any update of that particular factory that you showed me those images of last meeting?"
>
> If this is presented in a monitoring report or a dashboard, or the traffic light system which we always run through, there's no story behind that, no face behind the name of a factory in a province they've probably never been to in a town they have never been to. The image alone was enough to connect them. They may not have remembered the name of the factory, but they knew it was a factory in China and they saw some pictures they didn't like, and they want to know what has happened, and proactively.

I asked Sean whether lodging those images in their minds had any tangible results; he said he got a 15 percent budget increase the following year, though he couldn't prove that it was specifically due to those photographs.

Seeing those affected may be unusual for the C-suite, but many Corporate Idealists said it was vital for them. Darryl Knudsen, senior advisor on business and human rights at Gap Inc., told me of one particularly intimate encounter in early 2011, choking up as he did so:

One of the ways I keep myself honest on these things is by, whenever I can, making a choice to directly meet or talk to the people who are being impacted. I need to be confident in representing the choices we're making as a company and I need to know I'm going to fight hard for the right choices.

We went to Bangladesh in the immediate aftermath of a fire at a supplier, and I told my delegation I'm going to go to the hospital to meet the survivors. I learned on the way to the hospital how to say in Bengali, "I'm so sorry this happened to you." I said what company I was from; I told them, "If you want to tell your story I want to listen to it, but most importantly I want to tell you I'm so sorry that this happened to you." One person didn't want to talk, but everyone else did. They wanted to tell me what happened. One of them said, "We were having lunch in the canteen and the fire alarm went off. I thought it wasn't real and I wanted to finish my lunch and so I did, and then there was smoke everywhere." Another person said they were worried because there had been riots outside over wages so he didn't want to go out. They told me there were about 200 people on the top-floor canteen and that most left with the alarm. Of those that stayed, some made it out. Twenty-nine died.

They wanted to tell me about how they were groping through the smoke in the stairwells. One of them said he was sliding down a rope and his hands were burning and he showed me his hands and you could see how the skin was still gone, scarred. He said, "Someone landed on me and I let go and I remember waking up in a hospital." He had fallen eight stories onto the ground.

The hardest part was there were parents who were there. Their faces, they just looked like they had died. They just stared at me. Their faces are still with me.

So it's so important, right? You're out here having these policy discussions, and if it gets too abstract you can get lost. John Ruggie said it nicely in his book *Just Business*, about his time as U.N. Special Representative for business and human rights]: his heart would drive his commitment, but he needed to use his mind to be successful. I think that's absolutely right. You can't let go of the first part, though.

In the years after that, Darryl was deeply involved in discussions with the range of organizations working to improve labor conditions in Bangladesh, whose efforts stepped up considerably after the Rana Plaza disaster and a fire six months earlier at the Tazreen factory on the outskirts of Dhaka that killed 117 workers. Those discussions resulted in new commitments by brands and retailers to improve fire and building safety; Darryl told me that the factory that employed the workers he visited now has automatic fire-safe doors, sprinkler systems, and external fire exits, which it did not have before. "Throughout all of that work—which has been in turns invigorating, discouraging, and terrifying," he told me, "I kept the survivors' words and faces with me."

Michael Samway was a vice president and deputy general counsel at Yahoo! when the company faced criticism for complying with a Chinese law enforcement request for information used to identify journalist Shi Tao, who was then imprisoned for disclosing state secrets. In 2007 Yahoo!'s general counsel and CEO were called to testify before Congress, where California Representative Tom Lantos lambasted them: "While technologically and financially you are giants, morally you are pygmies."

Shortly after that Michael met with Shi's mother in Washington, D.C. Michael told me that, through a translator, he attempted to explain Yahoo!'s efforts to advocate for her son's release. He described her as gracious, even in her sadness. "She took my hand and said I looked the same age as her son. Whatever small amount of comfort I tried to give her, she returned equally with her nod of understanding." The encounter left a deep impression on Michael and reminded him of the high stakes of his industry. "It reinforced the complexity of the issues. We'd made a decision before any other major Internet company to offer potentially transformative information and communications services in a country that ultimately had a different conception of human rights."

The next year, Michael created Yahoo!'s Business and Human Rights Program and brought in a senior lawyer, Ebele Okobi, to run it. The program established a cross-functional team and spelled out guidelines for the company to assess and mitigate human rights risks, including a mandate to do human rights impact assessments (like the study I commissioned for BP in Indonesia) and external stakeholder engagement. Ebele told me: "I never had to make the pitch: 'We should do this, it's important, and this is why.' Yahoo! had been so beaten up, and it was a personal thrashing: Jerry was *personally* called a moral pygmy, our general counsel was *personally* called a perjurer. I never had to convince anybody that this is important work."

These cases and so many more demonstrate the urgency of the work of the Corporate Idealist. Many of the policies and practices that Corporate Idealists push for are not cosmetic and cannot wait another year, quarter, or even a month: peoples' lives are at stake. In many instances, CEOs see that urgency firsthand. Then the question remains: Why do these disasters keep happening?

Cost of Doing Business?

The harshest explanation is that some companies see such incidents as simply a cost of doing business. Sean Ansett said to me, "A very harsh view on this is you could, as a company, imagine doing a calculation and say there's going to be a major problem every two years, it will cost x amount, but we'll keep going forward with the business model, because that's what the shareholders require and what consumers are still demanding." Ford came under fire in the 1970s when it was reported that the company decided not to add a safety feature to the Pinto because it cost more than the $200,000 value that Ford set for a human life.

Even those companies not living explicitly by Ford's alleged 1970s model have to perform some sort of cost-benefit analysis. Since much of the Corporate Idealist's work is preventative and touches multifaceted issues with multiple levers, it can be hard to justify the expense of any one intervention. Disasters sometimes get a price tag put on them, like ExxonMobil's shutdown due to civil unrest in Aceh ($100 million to $350 million) and the Deepwater Horizon explosion ($42 billion and counting). One of my former colleagues on the U.N. mandate on business and human rights led a study showing that a major mine can lose $20 million for every week its production is delayed due to local conflicts.

While the dollar is mighty, it is not the only factor in driving behavior. As I saw in China and Indonesia, risks to reputation and social license to operate can be just as powerful.

No Rewards for What Doesn't Happen

Keeping risks front of mind without seeming alarmist is a critical but important task for Corporate Idealists, in part because their success is defined by crises not occurring, and people rarely get rewarded for something that doesn't happen. Like anyone playing defense, Corporate Idealists may have lots of saves, but history tends to remember the moments when they failed. One Corporate Idealist told me that she was livid when one of her company's prestigious internal awards went to a colleague who handled a major safety disaster. "Really?" she marveled. "What about those of us who made sure we didn't have any safety disasters?"

Ebele Okobi at Yahoo! told me: "A big part of what you do is prevent bad things from happening. So being good at your job means that people start thinking, 'Do we really need this?'"

Jonathan Drimmer, vice president and assistant general counsel at Barrick Gold, started rolling out a company-wide human rights training program in 2011. He said initially there was some resistance from staff having to take time to do the training, but that faded. I asked whether anyone actually complimented the training. He responded, "No one ever said, 'It's pretty good.' They just don't complain. The way that you know that it's gone well is if you don't hear about it."

Out of the Loop

Then there are the Corporate Idealists who are so marginalized they don't even know it. In 2012 I attended a talk by a man who headed corporate responsibility for a major investment bank, who talked about his organization's terrific philanthropic programs to give away a sliver of the bank's profits. In passing he mentioned getting invited onto a conference call with colleagues considering a deal involving a factory in Central America known to have caused serious environmental damage. He marveled at how strange it was that his colleagues would consider such a deal; I marveled that he seemed oblivious to the likelihood that there were probably hundreds of calls like that every week that he was *not* invited to.

For months after his talk I was seething about how delusional he was. How dare he talk about how great his institution is when they were such a key player in the financial crisis that brought down the global economy! And how naïve he must be to think that the few minutes per year he spends with the CEO is emblematic of how that executive runs the rest of the company with the rest of his time.

Then one day in the middle of one of my mental rants I thought, Wait a second: Am I that deluded as well? Do I sound just as ridiculous, talking about the great things BP has done on human rights on a few projects in far-flung corners of the world, when the company's behavior much closer to home appears to have been the opposite of exemplary?

Perhaps. But I still believe that my work was part of the company's core business, mitigating risk around critical projects, not an irrelevant stream of activity. If Mr. Socially Responsible Bank had blocked that proposed polluter project or at least instituted conditionality on the deal (like adherence to the Equator Principles, a standard for environmental and social performance that eighty banks around the world have signed up to), I would have been more forgiving. It is all too obvious now that I didn't reach every corner of BP, but I saw positive effects of my work on major projects, such as the absence of construction fatalities on the SECCO project in China and the community programs and relationships around the Tangguh project in Indonesia. But still, I have to wonder: Was I more marginalized than I realized?

This is a common question for the Corporate Idealist. One Corporate Idealist who is often wheeled out in crises to deal with angry activists told me, "I feel totally essential and completely marginalized." Anna Murray, founder of the group Young Women in Energy, told me "The overt things I can handle because at least it's direct. It's the covert, like those times when the role is not included as part of the discussion and overall planning. That is always the hardest part as it demonstrates a complete lack of understanding and respect for the function."

Even when colleagues get the issues, the Corporate Idealist still has to prove constructive enough to be brought to the table. "Because they have to want to invite you into the meeting," Monica Gorman of New Balance told me, "even if they don't particularly like what you're going to say."

The Corporate Idealist must constantly build internal relationships throughout the company—not just within his or her function, but across (business units, regions, and departments), up (to senior executives and the next generation of leaders), and out (to managers in the field and on the front lines). Human rights and sustainability encompass so many different issues that hardly any corner of a company is irrelevant, and the Corporate Idealist has to make sure that everyone knows that to prevent problems and engage in solutions. As Dan Bross, director of corporate citizenship at Microsoft, told me, "I have a horizontal job in a vertical world."

A Perfect Storm

I now recognize that the projects I worked on in Asia faced an extraordinary level of scrutiny from host and home governments, local and international NGOs, investors, and neighbors. On the other hand, the Presidential Oil Spill Commission report describes the U.S. Minerals Management Service, the agency with oversight responsibility for offshore drilling (which was overhauled after the spill), as "systematically lacking the resources, technical training, or experience in petroleum engineering that is absolutely critical to ensuring that offshore drilling is being conducted in a safe and responsible manner." The report goes onto say that "Presidents, members of Congress, and agency leadership had become preoccupied for decades with the enormous revenues generated by such drilling rather than focused on ensuring its safety." To translate the report into the language of the U.N. Guiding Principles on Business and Human Rights, in the Gulf of Mexico the U.S. government was not fulfilling its "duty to protect." Nor does there appear to have been a comparable level of NGO or local scrutiny in the gulf to what I experienced on other projects.

Not that a lack of external scrutiny should excuse bad behavior. As legendary UCLA basketball coach John Wooden said, "The true test of a man's character is what he does when no one is watching." In more formal terms, the U.N. Guiding Principles make clear that a company's responsibility to respect human rights exists regardless of whether the government is fulfilling its duties.

But historically institutions do not act as they should without external scrutiny, as Arvind Ganesan, director of Human Rights Watch's Business and Human Rights Division told me:

There is no evidence in history going back a hundred years of enlightened self-interest being the catalyst for companies or governments to regulate companies on human rights grounds. All you have to do is go back to antitrust law or Upton Sinclair's *The Jungle*, and you can see that every time there has been a law or regulation or practice that has been applied to companies that in effect has a human rights benefit—whether it's labor law or anything else—it is not due to progressive motivation by that institution. Rather, it's due to outside pressure.

Arvind explained that he sees his division's role as, first, to expose a problem: "to document it in an objective and thorough way, and bring it to public attention, and provide an analysis that provides a solution." But he also sees part of his role as helping Corporate Idealists and their counterparts in government do their jobs: "What NGOs do in all cases is create space for progressive voices inside the institutions to make changes." Meg Roggensack, who led business engagement for Human Rights First, agreed:

Largely, you are working to help empower people in companies to do these things. We can certainly make a mark on the outside and create pressures, that's important too. But ultimately, broadly we do have similar goals. We often need to reframe the issue to help them articulate our shared concerns and enable them to engage more effectively.

In the Tangguh project in Indonesia, it wasn't just external scrutiny that made us take the extraordinary measures that we did. It was a perfect confluence of factors: a chief executive who had just gone through an operational and reputational crisis in Colombia and didn't want to make the same mistakes again; a few BP executives who moved directly to Indonesia from Colombia and saw firsthand the importance of securing the social license to operate; delays securing buyers for the gas, which allowed time to deepen our understanding of the context and strengthen local relationships; and a setting that was so obviously unique and sensitive in so many ways that it demanded nothing short of every imaginable effort.

In China I was in a similarly sensitive environment, with BP executives keen to establish good relationships and protocols with what would hopefully be a long-term partner and joint venture partners who valued their reputation, and physical proximity to a major international city and media market. The BP colleagues who participated so enthusiastically in my human rights work in London were coming from projects that also demanded heightened attention. But they were, I now realize, only part of the company's global staff.

Let's assume that the case is made by a crisis, pressure, or otherwise, and the Corporate Idealist wins a seat at the grown-ups' table. Now what? It's one thing to raise awareness of complex issues, but what can Corporate Idealists and their companies do about them?

Wish List

On the typical Corporate Idealist wish list is incorporation of social issues into resource allocation and project approval processes, for example not sending a project into its next stage of development until social risks have been assessed; license and budget to collaborate with peer companies and engage with nongovernmental organizations and directly affected communities; and permission to communicate more openly about the company's challenges. A number of Corporate Idealists told me that their biggest hurdles are their Communications Departments, who want only to publish good stories; whereas Corporate Idealists argue that a more nuanced discussion of challenges has greater credibility and opens up space for collaboration.

The Corporate Idealist wish list is hardly radical, but each item can represent a departure from the usual way of doing business. Sometimes it takes one company to move first, then others can follow suit. A number of Corporate Idealists in different industries told me they had to fight hard internally to publish their supplier lists, against colleagues' perceptions that doing so would somehow put them at a competitive disadvantage, even though Nike and Levi-Strauss published their lists in 1995 and HP led the electronics industry by doing so in 2008. Still, many Corporate Idealists told me that they didn't win until a close peer company—comparable in size, market, and supplier base—published its list and their colleagues saw that, as one person put it to me, "the world did not end."

Jeffrey Hollender, cofounder and former CEO of Seventh Generation, the popular green brand of household products, told me that he sees demonstrating what is possible as a big part of his mission:

> I've become increasingly focused on building models of new possibilities that hopefully will A) prove they're possible; B) inspire others to follow; and C) begin people asking the question that if one business can do it, then why are other businesses not behaving in that way. That is where Seventh Generation was

most successful: it inspired other companies to emulate many of our practices. The Seventh Generation model clearly lays out for consumers what they should or could expect from us. It wasn't a good enough model, but it was better than much of the alternative.

The value of my role as a businessperson is that I stand from a place in conversations with other businesses that enables me to challenge their behavior because I have successfully pursued a different path. It's different when I stand up and speak as the chair of Greenpeace about corporate behavior than when I stand up and speak as a business leader.

After its crisis in China, Yahoo! demonstrated how to implement a number of items on the Corporate Idealist wish list, with the company's Business and Human Rights Program, led by Ebele Okobi, now routinely conducting human rights impact assessments and proactively engaging with human rights activists.

Ecosystem

Yet the work of Ebele and other Corporate Idealists shows the limits of what one company can do alone. Companies are subject to the laws of the countries in which they operate, and violating them can present serious risks to their employees and their businesses. A few Corporate Idealists told me about staff getting harassed and even detained for challenging government orders, but wouldn't go on the record for fear of further antagonizing their regulators and endangering their colleagues. BP was threatened with expropriation after committing to publish its payments to the Angolan government.

Even if pushing back on laws had no consequences, companies cannot be left to decide that compliance is optional. Internet companies have come under fire for complying with government requests around the world for user information, but they don't know whether a request is for jailing a dissident or tracking down a bomb. As Ebele told me:

> People don't understand the risks to employees, and people also act as if following the law in a country is optional. You don't actually want that. You do not want companies, with employees who have not been elected by anyone, who represent no collective interest apart from shareholders, setting themselves above or beyond the law. You don't want, for example, a Chinese company coming to the U.S. and saying, "Yes, yes, we know about your First Amendment and your labor laws, but we're just going to do our own thing."

It is impossible to separate the actions and potential of a multinational corporation from the ecosystem that it is part of, which includes government laws and practices (which can contradict each other), civil society, individual customers and citizens, and the international community. Each of the issues that Corporate Idealists come across is complex enough on its own, but the issues are also interconnected.

In Indonesia, I learned that BP's security couldn't be arranged without considering the company's and the military's relationship with local communities; which couldn't be considered in isolation from those communities' health and well-being; which depended on their geography, history, and relationship with local, provincial, and national governments; which was shaped by the state of the nation's economy and politics. The company's role in all of that would be shaped in part by the latest technical possibilities for how the company could help meet regional and global energy demand while causing minimal disruption to the physical and social surroundings of the resource.

Staying competitive in the apparel industry for big brands has come to mean sourcing in the country where wages are lowest. But as Rana Plaza tragically demonstrated, garment worker wages are only one small piece of the puzzle. As Jeremy Prepscius of BSR told me: "Wages are one part. But wages also include the wages of the health and safety manager, the wages of the human resources manager, the wages of the guy who built the building. You're buying the whole shebang."

As much complexity as there is at the production end of the supply chain, the consumption end of course shapes corporate practices too. Some studies show that ensuring good working conditions would add less than one dollar to the price of a pair of blue jeans. But other studies show that any premium will send customers elsewhere. Despite responding to surveys that they care about ethics, shoppers refuse to pay more. In one study only half of customers chose a pair of socks marked "Good Working Conditions" even when they were the same price as an unmarked pair; only one quarter of customers paid for the socks when they cost 50 percent more.

Understanding the systemic complexity helps form a realistic view of one's role in it. Darryl Knudsen, senior advisor on business and human rights at Gap Inc., told me: "I have fewer crises of confidence now than I used to. I don't know if that's good or bad. I don't take things as personally as I used to and I don't feel as much personal responsibility to solve everything as I used to, as much sole responsibility. It is really a case of a much broader system, and we've each got to do our part." He said a colleague once told him that "the problem is not that any one individual, organization, or company has too much power; it's that nobody's at the wheel."

Realizing that the issues we work on are complex and systemic is daunting. So how do Corporate Idealists view their work and set expectations that are realistic but still worthwhile?

Saving One Finger at a Time

Many of the Corporate Idealists I spoke with recognized that their work is incremental. They're not overthrowing capitalism or their companies, nor are they even preventing people from getting hurt on their watch. But they do believe that they are slowly moving their supertanker companies in the right direction.

Monica Gorman of New Balance told me: "I wouldn't do this if I didn't think that we were making it better. Is it so incremental you can barely see it sometimes? Definitely." In the four years in her previous role, as head of corporate responsibility and international trade compliance at American Eagle Outfitters, she helped pilot a worker hotline in China, led the company to join the Fair Labor Association, and issued their first corporate social responsibility report. She acknowledged that other more advanced companies may not consider those steps groundbreaking, but "it took time to build the comfort level and the fluency to be able to do that. I feel like that's made a difference; there are a lot more people in this company who know about these issues than three-and-a-half years ago. So that's what keeps you going. But you realize how far you have to go."

Charlotte Grezo has worked in sustainability in the energy, telecoms, and financial sectors, and takes a very pragmatic view of her work: "Whether they were doing enough or doing things in the best way is always open to interpretation. But at least they were far less likely to make major mistakes and behave badly than when I arrived."

Dave Stangis told me about his company, Campbell's Soup, making it onto the Dow Jones Sustainability Index: "That's what keeps us here, right? Those little wins make our day. There will always be things that we don't do as well as we could, frankly, and there are many things that I continue to learn from watching other companies, and there are some things that I know we lead in. But we've got a long way to go. Sustainability is an ultra-marathon and the finish line is always moving."

Kevin Hagen was corporate responsibility manager for REI, the outdoor clothing and gear retailer, from 2008 to 2012. He said in an interview with GreenBiz.com about his time with the company:

A lot of folks talk about incremental improvements as being not good enough, because slowing down the car on its way toward the cliff—from [green design guru] Bill McDonough's metaphor—isn't the right approach. However, by working on incremental improvements, we train the organization in new ways. We learn new skills, new competencies, and that opened our eyes to breakthrough opportunities as we started working on a new aspect—say, energy efficiency—and started making improvements. But then we realized that we could actually do things completely differently, like power the store from solar, and that was a breakthrough kind of thing.

So I think that incremental improvements are really important, even if they're not sufficient, because they set the organization up for understanding what real breakthroughs might be.

Incrementalism can mean taking small organizational steps toward a big goal—or focusing on one person at a time. Marcela Manubens worked in social responsibility for two decades in the apparel industry and is now global vice president for social impact at Unilever. She told me about her first visit to Bangladesh in the 1990s. Flying in during monsoon season when there had been major flooding, she could see families huddling on rooftops waiting to be rescued. In the arrivals lounge of the airport, a woman shoved a baby into Marcela's arms; her guide explained that the woman was offering Marcela her child for sale.

Marcela had traveled widely but never seen as much poverty as she saw that day, and arrived at her hotel that night in tears. She told herself: "Marcela, calm down, just one life, just one person. If I impact one person, I'm fine. That's how I started looking at our work: one person at a time."

Jeremy Prepscius of BSR sees incrementalism—which we discussed as saving one finger from industrial accidents at a time—as necessary but not sufficient: "If all of this has no earth-shattering impact, if it's tactical and operational and it's about individual fingers and toes, I'm fine with that. But that's not what this should do. Because what we are actually talking about here is the fundamental question of our age: How does a global business operate?"

Looking for Transformation

My former BP colleague David Rice retired from the company in 2006 and is now a fellow with the University of Cambridge Programme for Sustainability Leadership. He teaches and mentors professionals from a wide range of industries and sees many people take on an incremental view, which he described as "'I may work for a company that I'm not entirely sure about, but I think I'm making it better than it would have been.' That can be very satisfying."

But David was also part of bringing about industry shifts. After BP struggled to devise appropriate security arrangements in Colombia and realized it could not and should not write rules on its own, David helped form a coalition of companies, human rights groups, and governments to develop the Voluntary Principles on Security and Human Rights, which most of the major extractive companies have signed onto. BP's controversial attempts to publish its government payments in Angola helped bring about the Extractive Industries Transparency Initiative (EITI), which now counts twenty-three countries as compliant with its principles and eighty of the world's largest oil, gas, and mining companies as supporters. David told me:

> The thing I feel most pleased about is I think we changed the entire industry—through the Voluntary Principles, through EITI, through carbon trading. [BP's internal emissions trading program was one of the predecessors to the European Union's program.] Any one company can go backwards, but they can't undo that. You make these incremental changes, but at some point you can do something transformational—transform your industry

and sector. Then you've affected people's lives in many parts of the world.

Moving an industry is not just satisfying; it's essential to address some of these complex issues that no one company can or should address alone. When Doug Cahn ran the human rights program for Reebok, he led the effort to ensure that no child labor went into making the company's soccer balls, which was no small feat given the extent of child labor in Sialkot, Pakistan, where most soccer balls were made at the time. Reebok proudly printed on the balls "Guaranteed manufactured without child labor." However, Doug said, "We did have at least one retailer tell us they didn't want to buy our balls because we implied that all the other balls on the shelves made by our competitors were made with child labor—and they didn't want to go there." Reebok eventually rallied the Sporting Goods Manufacturers Association and the World Federation of Sporting Goods Industry to commit to higher standards for all of its members—and pulled its own label.

But some Corporate Idealists lose patience for toiling away at incrementalism while waiting for those rare opportunities for transformation. Jeffrey Hollender founded Seventh Generation and over two decades grew it into a leading green brand of consumer goods. But he got disillusioned and eventually left the company. He told me why:

> It became increasingly clear that we, the so-called "socially responsible," "sustainable" business community are pursuing a paradigm of being less bad and don't really have an understanding of what "good" is. Whenever you make a paper towel, even if it's made from recycled material and unbleached, you're still

contributing to a whole host of environmental negative impacts that will continue to keep us on this road that we're on. It set me off on a really different path, which was what does it mean to be good and regenerative.

In some way, "sustainability" is problematic because even if we sustain the state we're in, we're not going to address the problems that we're facing. It was a sad realization that with all the work we had done, what we really managed to do was create products that are less bad than competitors' products.

Having one of the leaders of sustainability challenge the whole notion of sustainability is enough to give any Corporate Idealist pause. Similarly, after thirteen years working on supply chains for Gap Inc., Burberry, and Apple, Sean Ansett told me that he asked himself, "Do I continue working largely on incrementalism, or do I want to spend the next fifteen years on more transformative stuff?" He has chosen the latter, taking on a few social enterprise projects and becoming chief sustainability officer for Fairphone, whose mission is to create the first smartphone "that puts social values first" by using conflict-free resources and paying fair wages.

But other Corporate Idealists choose to stay in big companies, which Sean respects: "I think people have to make both a professional and personal choice on this, and there are some very passionate and hardworking folks pushing boundaries. There is room for incrementalism and we need people working on that. We need people at the global level working on policy and frameworks. We need boots on the ground and everything in between."

When I asked Doug Cahn, formerly of Reebok, whether he thought that we should work to improve the complex and flawed supply chain system we have today or create a new one from scratch, he replied: "The answer to that question has been different for me at different points along the road, and so I am open to the possibility that it will change again. Are there limitations today that we knew about ten years ago? You bet. There are also opportunities as well. If we fail to engage in incremental steps at the same time that we strive for different supply chain relationships, then the workers we seek to protect could be harmed along the way. I don't see these as binary."

I had never thought about incrementalism or perceived my work as such until numerous Corporate Idealists brought it up to me. It helped me better understand my time with BP. I did not reach every person in every asset in the company, but I did make meaningful changes on a few important projects and helped a number of colleagues do the same. I piloted specific good practices, such as a human rights impact assessment, that other companies could then emulate. I was also part of broader initiatives, such as with the United Nations, that brought about change beyond any individual company.

Given the breadth and complexity of the issues at stake, I should be more heartened by my contribution than I felt in the wake of events that seemed to undermine it. As Helen Keller said, "The world is moved along, not only by the mighty shoves of its heroes, but also by the aggregate of tiny pushes of each honest worker."

Helen Keller's quote is apt to support the idea of incrementalism, but I am uncomfortable evoking comparisons between Helen Keller—a historic pioneer and champion for people with disabilities—and Corporate Idealists. Faris Natour spent four years as an analyst at Calvert Investments before joining BSR, where he leads the human rights practice, working with companies across industries. He warned:

We need to be careful about not being overly congratulatory to all of us in CSR, thinking that we are the only true champions of human rights. We are idealists inside the business world, but to human rights advocates outside of business, we are pragmatists. We may be idealistic on a personal level, and we serve an important role—but that role is based on compromise, practicality, and frankly also a desire to have a comfortable perch from which to advocate for human rights.

We need to honor the true idealists, human rights defenders around the world who seek to hold business accountable, many risking arrest and persecution, without the comfort of a corporate salary, a 401k, and a posh office.

Those who put their lives on the line to protect others should absolutely be honored—and paid more. But just as Corporate Idealists should not be smug, nor should we apologize. Dan Pallotta became an outspoken critic of the view that people who make money can't be committed to social justice after attracting criticism for earning a $394,500 salary organizing charitable events like the AIDSRides. He said in a TED talk:

We have a visceral reaction to the idea that anyone would make very much money helping other people. Interesting that we don't have a visceral reaction to the notion that people would make a lot of money *not* helping other people. You want to make $50 million selling violent video games to kids, go for it. We'll put you on the cover of *Wired* magazine. But you want to make half a million dollars trying to cure kids of malaria, and you're considered a parasite yourself.

We think of this as our system of ethics, but what we don't realize is that this system has a powerful side effect, which is, it gives a really stark, mutually exclusive choice between doing very well for yourself and your family or doing good for the world to the brightest minds coming out of our best universities, and sends tens of thousands of people who could make a huge difference in the nonprofit sector marching every year directly into the for-profit sector because they're not willing to make that kind of lifelong economic sacrifice.

Corporate Idealists earn a decent salary while committing to one of the most critical challenges of our time: how to make big business work in our best interests. I wish we lived in a world where public school teachers and human rights defenders were paid more. But I also want corporations to spend money on salaries and budgets to improve the impacts of their business on people and the environment, and I want some of the world's brightest minds to be on the receiving end of those funds.

Supping with the Devil

At the launch of the U.N. Global Compact corporate responsibility initiative, then-Secretary-General Kofi Annan was asked whether sharing the dais with Phil Knight of Nike, who had been demonized by anti-sweatshop campaigners, wasn't like supping with the devil. Annan replied: "The angels don't need our help." As Aron Cramer, president and CEO of BSR (Business for Social Responsibility), told me: "The trick is to get them to the table, then move the table." Bill McDonough wrote in *Cradle to Cradle*, one of the bibles of the environmental movement:

> 'How can you work with *them*?' we are often asked, regarding our willingness to work with every sector of the economy, including big corporations. To which we sometimes reply, 'How can you *not* work with them?' (We think of Emerson visiting Thoreau when he was jailed for not paying his taxes—part of his civil disobedience. 'What are you doing in there?' Emerson is said to have asked, prompting Thoreau's famous retort: 'What are you doing out there?')

Some people express discomfort at the notion of working *with* companies; working *inside* them, as Corporate Idealists have chosen to do, can be even harder to embrace. Liesel Filgueiras told me that when she joined Vale, the Brazilian mining company, a friend asked, "How do you feel being on the 'dark side of the force'?" She replied:

> It is not a matter of good or bad; I feel like I can do so much more from the inside. Being part of the company allows me to avoid problems and work on proactive risk management, something that if you are in an external institution like a NGO you cannot do. You will only be able to deal with the impact and problems that already happened and escalated.

As an example of proactive risk management, Liesel told me that Vale was considering locating a dormitory near an indigenous community, which would have caused social tensions. But her team successfully argued for a different site, much to her satisfaction:

> That's where I feel most powerful and most rewarded is in this invisible work, when we are able to avoid problems. This will not be measured; it will not be rewarded in any material way. But I know it was extremely important for the company and for the community, and everybody that participated in this decision knows. This is a very, very important part of our role inside the company.

A few Corporate Idealists told me they had trouble adjusting to being on the inside. Gillian Davidson joined Teck Resources, the Canadian mining company, after stints in academia and government. She told me that one night she ended up in a heated argument with old friends at a pub over her company's water usage in areas of Chile where there are no major rivers and minimal rainfall:

> My voice has changed in conversation—not in a way I always like. I've gone from using the first person and the "I" and "this is my experience of it and what I think about it" to the royal "We" and defending the company. I took a step back and said, "What does this mean? It doesn't mean you sold out, or has it? Am I still questioning internally to the extent that I should be?"
>
> I remember it was getting more heated. I thought, what am I getting defensive about? It's the way I used to feel passionate when I'm arguing for communities, that I hope I still do when I'm in the organization.

We've made big changes, culture change and trans-formational change within operations. It's not a quick job. It's not an easy job. I had this realization that I am getting defensive because it's not just "we." The con-versation is about the "we" but I realized I owned part of that story. My part might be small, but I'm proud of what I've done within that storyline.

Gillian and I both questioned whether inside a company is the right place to be; these struggles are not only typical, but healthy. Darrell Doren, global compliance director of Avery Dennison, told me, "I can really get behind the person that says, 'Here are the reasons that we do what we do, and this is why we struggle.' The rabbinical literature and Buddhist literature indi-cate that your faith is a struggle. It's not delivered to you; it's not *ab initio* just handed over to you as it is with certain religions. It's something that you have to fight with, and it's something you have to struggle with."

Ebele Okobi, who runs the Business and Human Rights Program at Yahoo!, told me about her struggle:

In order to do this work well you have to care deeply about the company, and you have to believe that the company wants to do the right thing, even if it's not always readily apparent to people outside. Once you stop believing that there is a critical mass of people in the company who are committed to responsible engage-ment, however, then you have to ask yourself why you are there—are you really making a difference, or are you doing P.R.? P.R. is useful, but at most companies P.R. isn't making strategic operational decisions. So you have to ask yourself: "Is this where I want to be?"

The other tricky thing is that you are neither fish nor fowl; I am an outsider on the inside, and an insider on the outside. It is at once incredibly energizing, and on some days incredibly lonely work. Along with caring about and believing in your company, you have to be less concerned about your own personal advancement in order to do this job well. If you're doing it right, at any given moment someone, somewhere, is deeply pissed at you.

I asked one of the human rights advocates whom I've known for years whether she could ever see herself working in a company. She said:

I don't know that I could overcome my sense that I would have to accept that I was part of whatever the abuses were, even if I was trying to fix them internally. That I was still going to be identified with them, not just externally to people but in myself; that I was going to feel like I was somehow responsible or implicated in them, and that was something I didn't think I could live with.

Yet she didn't want her name associated with that quote, since she believes that companies can do good work, and part of her hopes that she might someday find a company that she could work for without feeling like she had to compromise.

Compromise is inevitable in the work of the Corporate Idealist—but certainly is not unique to corporate life. Joanne Bauer, a human rights advocate and scholar at Columbia University (with whom I began coteaching a course on human rights and business in 2012) told me:

Activists must also operate within their own institutional constraints and make choices all the time about when and when not to compromise: be it in their selection of issues to go after, how to cover them, when to go public with allegations and when to engage, when to join a coalition or multistakeholder initiative and when not to, when to sustain a campaign and when to move on, and how to deal with donors for whom certain subjects are taboo.

Darryl Knudsen of Gap Inc. shared with me thoughts he prepared for an aspiring Corporate Idealist: "Making progress as a CSR professional is slow but steady work, like a river eroding rock. You can make real progress against the most intractable social problems, but there are some issues that you will never be able to touch from the vantage of your company."

For a long time after the Deepwater Horizon disaster, I didn't think I had the stomach for corporate work—at least not the work tackling the challenges at the core of the business, which is the only kind of work I wanted to do. I felt like my anonymous advocate friend who didn't want to be part of a company that could be linked to problems, no matter how hard she was trying to solve them.

But the more I spoke with others about the small wins that make a difference to the company and beyond and the importance of having change agents on the inside, the more I rediscovered my Corporate Idealism. Accepting that this work is incremental and that crises will continue to happen—while not accepting that those crises are inevitable—allowed me to once again embrace the work I had done and recommit to the field wholeheartedly. Never again will I develop such a crush on a company that I am blind to its faults. I now know the dangers and pitfalls of working in and with big companies toward more responsible practices, but also see its possibilities with less of a rose-colored tint.

My renewed commitment is backed up by an even stronger sense of urgency. The global community needs Corporate Idealists: not to order matching T-shirts for employees to wear as they paint a fence for five hours a year like some "CSR" or "corporate citizenship" jobs entail, but to make sure that disasters like the Rana Plaza factory collapse and the Deepwater Horizon disaster are the shocking, catalytic, black swan events that they are rather than the norm.

As economist Paul Romer said, "A crisis is a terrible thing to waste." After the Rana Plaza factory collapse Gare Smith, the lawyer who carried out the human rights impact assessment for BP's Tangguh project in Indonesia, was retained by the Bangladeshi government to advise on how best to promote respect for workers' rights. Gare draws a parallel to the 1911 Triangle Shirtwaist Factory fire: "Nothing got fixed overnight, but it helped spawn the modern labor rights movement and changed the manner in which business is conducted." Corporate Idealists and advocates I've spoken with are cautiously optimistic that Rana Plaza is generating action on the part of governments, companies, and the labor movement that will add up to meaningful change. Even so, I don't think that even the most optimistic among them believes that there will never be another factory accident.

The Deepwater Horizon disaster sparked overhaul of offshore drilling regulation, but that won't be enough on its own to prevent future crises in that industry. All parts of our global ecosystem need to act individually and in concert: companies must recognize that what is good for society is good for their business; investors must recognize that the way companies manage externalities is probably indicative of how they manage other issues; NGOs must exercise their roles as researchers, watchdogs, advocates, and partners; workers and communities must know and exercise their rights; consumers must realize that cheap goods have hidden costs; and the media and regulators must be vigilant and proactive. Amidst all of that, Corporate Idealists must keep working toward both incremental and transformative change. To do so, they need persistence, confidence, and a strong community of peers.

Chapter 6

NEW YORK: COMMUNITY AND CAREERS

In September 2012, I gave birth to a healthy set of twins. Just over six weeks later I managed to shower, put on a clean set of clothes and two matching shoes, and take the subway to midtown Manhattan for my Corporate Idealist family reunion.

The gathering is officially known as the annual conference put on by BSR, formerly Business for Social Responsibility, the twenty-year-old nonprofit that works with its global network of more than two hundred fifty companies and other organizations on a wide range of sustainability issues. I began following BSR's work when I started at BP, and joined them part-time as a human rights advisor after the U.N. mandate ended in 2011.

Not much else could have gotten me out of the house and I could barely string a sentence together, but I didn't want to miss the chance to be in the presence of so many other Corporate Idealists. Stanford Business School professor Debra Meyerson writes about "Tempered Radicals," whom she describes as people "who want to succeed in their organizations yet want to live by their values or identities, even if they are somehow at odds with the dominant culture of their organizations... They want to rock the boat, and they want to stay in it." She includes people working on social and environmental responsibility inside big corporations in her studies, and notes the importance of community:

> Tempered radicals are individual actors, yet they *depend on connections to others*...
>
> [T]hose relationships are essential to keep tempered radicals going, to help them affirm their sense of self, to aid them in their efforts to broaden their impact, and to forge collectives when necessary to drive larger institutional change. Perhaps most important, relationships prevent isolation and loneliness—a fate that all too often saps the energy and effectiveness of many tempered radicals.

Or, as popular author Seth Godin wrote in his book *Tribes*: "Human beings can't help it: we need to belong."

For the Corporate Idealist, being part of a community is critical for both personal and substantive reasons, as Meyerson points out. It can be isolating being the sole or primary champion for social issues in a big company, and connecting with others doing similar work provides moral support and new fuel for both individual and collaborative efforts.

Liz Maw is the CEO of Net Impact, the nonprofit that engages students and professionals who are passionate about using their careers to champion social and environmental change. Liz told me that building community is a primary goal of Net Impact's annual conference (which attracted 2,500 attendees in 2013) and the organization as a whole:

We try to build that community across employers so people can connect with others at different companies who are working on similar issues. While someone may feel alone in driving sustainability forward at their company, we help them discover that there are actually many others who can offer support, ideas, and pep talks.

We've had professionals say to us that they go to the Net Impact conference once a year for a burst of energy that keeps them going for the rest of the year. The conference does this through a great combination of inspiring stories plus a feeling that you are part of a massive volume of people working towards similar goals. Sustainability professionals often feel like they're an outlier in the rest of their lives, so seeing all of these people who want to do this kind of work is really encouraging.

I saw this firsthand in the Voluntary Principles for Security and Human Rights, the Global Network Initiative, the Business Leaders Initiative on Human Rights, and other efforts that brought people from different organizations together. The meetings were ostensibly about a particular issue, but the same people kept coming back every quarter because they left with a more purposeful to-do list and renewed energy to tackle it. In a blog post previewing BSR's 2013 conference, the theme of which was "The Power of Networks," BSR president and CEO Aron Cramer wrote, "The age of networks has also reshaped our mindsets, sparking new approaches to problem-solving that bring unusual partners together... Our ability to activate human, organizational, and technological networks may well be the ultimate test of our ability to achieve the vision of a truly just and sustainable world."

Sean Ansett, a veteran of Gap Inc., Apple, and Burberry, told me:

> Forums like BSR and even what's happening at a city level, where people doing this kind of work get together for a drink once a month, is really important. You need that support and forum to generate ideas, because anyone that claims to be an expert in this is a liar—none of us are yet! We need constant input and insight into what has worked and what hasn't and where we're headed. A lot of that is happening in conferences, pubs, and cafés around the world.

Darryl Knudsen, senior advisor on business and human rights at Gap Inc., told me about a conversation he had with another Corporate Idealist:

> He told me, 'We are all sustainability warriors. Sometimes one of us is injured and needs assistance and we need to be there for each other.' Maybe I'm sympathetic to it because my dad was in the military, but I think he is right. We wrestle with the same things, and we help each other out. I get my energy in this idea that it's a bigger project—bigger than any one of us.

Laura Rubbo at Disney told me: "I freely bother my peers in other companies all the time. I also freely accept their phone calls because this work is not easy and you do need to talk with others: What do they do, how they get to that conclusion, what has worked and what hasn't, and how is that similar or different to what might work in your company?" She describes this community as "a lot of highly dedicated, smart, passionate people who want to use the power of their business to improve people's lives. I take pride in knowing them and learning from them and being a part of that community."

Laura was at a meeting of the Global Social Compliance Program, a collaborative initiative of a few dozen companies working to improve conditions in their supply chains, when news broke of the 2012 Tazreen factory fire in Bangladesh, which killed more than one hundred people. Laura was thankful to be there at that terrible moment: "It was good to be with colleagues and be able to talk with them face to face: Are you in the factory? What are you seeing? What will we do next? That's the beauty of some of these forums: you talk about long-term strategic issues, but when incidents happen you're already working with the people you need to address the situation."

I facilitate BSR's human rights working group, which brings together companies from different industries for quarterly meetings to help them integrate human rights into their operations. They get no stamp of approval for participating, so they are there to learn, share, and connect. My BSR staff colleagues research standards and best practices while I focus on the facilitation, making sure that the meetings are interactive and that participants have plenty of time to talk one-on-one and in small groups. When I was with BP and the U.N. mandate I preferred to do research by asking peers what they had done rather than reading studies or reports; reports often presented ten-step plans that oversimplified, whereas peers told me what resistance I would encounter when those plans hit the real world. My aim in building community with the working group is that its members have plenty of those peers to call upon.

Career Paths

In 2009 I got overwhelmed by the volume of e-mails I was receiving from friends of friends and contacts of contacts interested in learning about corporate social responsibility, so I started holding conference calls to field the inquiries together. At first it was purely an attempt at efficiency, but I quickly realized that the calls build community and pool our collective knowledge, and consequently are more helpful to participants than one-on-one conversations.

The same questions arise over and over on these calls, from students as well as mid-career switchers: How do I get a job in corporate responsibility? Are my skills and interests a good fit for the field? And whether explicit or implied is always the million-dollar question: Will I be doing meaningful work or superficial public relations?

BSR and the Business and Human Rights Resource Centre post jobs on their websites relevant to their subject matter. Beyond those specialized sites, it can be hard to find the true Corporate Idealist jobs—the ones focused on the challenges at the heart of the business—since depending on the industry they might be in procurement, privacy, safety, or any number of other functions, making them difficult to search for.

The absence of a single clear label presents a challenge that is actually a blessing. First, there are so many kinds of roles that can positively shape a big company's impact that there should be opportunities for Corporate Idealists of many different skill sets. Law, consulting, and even accounting firms are developing CSR and sustainability practices. A number of people on my conference calls say, "I want to get into CSR"; my first question back to them is "Okay, but what do you want to *do*?" My career so far has involved traipsing around villages, setting up partnerships with nonprofits, managing expert studies, developing internal policies and procedures, and internal and external communications in various forms. What skills are priorities to develop and strengthen?

Secondly and perhaps more importantly, a job with a "CSR" or "sustainability" or "human rights" label may not be the right one for someone looking to gain increasing influence in a company. Every company is different, but Ellen Weinreb, one of the first recruiters to focus on sustainability, sees an overall trend away from those labels. Ellen told me that when she started her practice in the mid-2000s she was hired to recruit senior CSR professionals by companies seeking "a certain level of expertise that they weren't able to find easily, meaning that there were plenty of eager MBAs who said they wanted to do this work or might have had a three-month internship, but there weren't that many people who had started up and run a program." But now she is seeing companies embed sustainability in other corporate functions, so the CSR specialist roles are more junior. "The sustainability office is going away. It doesn't mean that sustainability is going away, but it means that the stand-alone siloed office is now being integrated." Integration is good news for sustainability, but can make it more challenging for Corporate Idealists to find a role.

As for that million-dollar question about whether a Corporate Idealist job will be truly impactful, that requires asking: What are the greatest tensions that the core business of this company and industry have with the best interests of society? Is this job addressing any of those? Where does the job report into? What authority does it have? The answers might not be set in stone and could be shaped by the right person—but they are worth keeping in mind.

I would also inquire why the role was created: Has the company gone through a crisis, like Yahoo! in China before hiring Ebele Okobi to run the Business and Human Rights Program, or The Coca-Cola Company in Colombia before hiring Ed Potter to direct Global Workplace Rights? Has one of its peer companies gone through a crisis? Is there a new CEO? The answers may or may not prove significant, but they can indicate where both support and resistance might come from.

Corporate Idealist career paths can take on various forms, but are almost always nonlinear. The Corporate Idealists I spoke with all came to their work from different directions.

Early Inklings

Some Corporate Idealists see hints of their work in their childhoods. At the age of ten, Ed Potter saw that the migrant workers on his older cousin's grape farm in western New York State were sleeping in their cars. He leveraged his paper route earnings to coax money out of his father and other relatives, and over the subsequent three years enlisted his cousins to help build family housing for the workers. Fifty years later, he would still be working on labor rights—for The Coca-Cola Company.

Ebele Okobi at Yahoo! told me, "Even as a little person, I wanted to do work that had meaning. My parents sacrificed and traveled oceans to come to the United States, so I owe. I stand on the shoulders of giants, and part of the deal is that I have a duty to give back to make the world a better place."

After law school, Ebele joined a big law firm and loved her *pro bono* work with political asylees, domestic violence victims, and artists, so took a year off to volunteer with nonprofit organizations with the vague intention of returning to corporate law. On September 11th, 2001, she lost one of her best friends, who worked for Cantor Fitzgerald, and realized that life was too short to return to a job she didn't love. After a few years in the nonprofit sector, including working on health-care advocacy and women's equality in the workplace, she became "increasingly fascinated and inspired by the power that corporations have to effect social change and transform nations, both in positive and negative ways." She earned her MBA and joined Nike, then couldn't believe her eyes when in 2008 she saw the opening to run Yahoo!'s new Business and Human Rights Program on BSR's website:

> I had a very peripatetic career. I was a corporate lawyer, worked for nonprofits, worked in marketing and business development, and as a consultant. I love my career but I know a lot of people would not appreciate the detours. And this was a job where they were *looking* for detours. Most importantly, they were looking for someone who would have a direct impact on critical corporate decisions—not P.R., not someone to greenwash what they were doing. It was an incredible opportunity!

Five years later, she still feels that way—albeit with many of the same ups and downs that I and our fellow Corporate Idealists experience—describing herself in an e-mail to me as "(slightly) bloody and (mostly) unbowed."

Early Experiences

Other Corporate Idealists trace their work back to early professional experiences. Monique Oxender was teaching environmental science at a public high school in the Midwest, and proposed a project for her students to study the impacts of a local research and development facility on the area's water quality. But the local school board rejected the proposal, saying it might anger the company that was so important to their community and tax base. Monique was stunned that even the possibility of antagonizing a company could scuttle an educational project, especially since her study might have found that the company was doing good work. She points to that as the moment when the seed was planted in her mind about the power of the private sector.

In graduate school at the University of Michigan she studied coffee supply chains, originally from an ecological perspective, but three months on a coffee farm in Mexico convinced her to include the human aspects of the industry. A project assessing General Motors' volunteer program led to an internship with Ford in its purchasing organization, which turned into a full-time job. After eight years at Ford Monique's career has come full circle, and she's back working with the coffee industry as senior director of sustainability at Green Mountain Coffee Roasters.

Monica Gorman wanted to be the first female secretary of state until Madeline Albright beat her to it. She realized while in graduate school for international affairs that the academic life was not for her, and business held some intrigue: "As I was studying the European Union, examining the political and legal drivers of economic integration, I saw that it was actually many private corporate actors that drove the political process. I had this 'Eureka!' moment of realizing that corporations are very influential on the world stage in influencing political and historic events."

Monica spent the last months of graduate school in 2003

trying to convince a company to hire her. She talked her way into a role with Gap Inc., where she was charged with coming up with an innovative way to report on its social responsibility efforts. The following year Gap published a CSR report, believed to be the first social responsibility report by any retailer. The report won accolades for "risking unprecedented honesty in reporting on factory conditions." An article in the *MIT Sloan Management Review* said:

> The "warts and all" report focused on code of conduct violations regarding labor rights and the supply chain and the measures being taken to prevent future violations. Although some media outlets interpreted the report as an act of contrition (with headlines like "Gap Admits to Running Sweatshops"), some of Gap's toughest critics praised the effort... In public relations terms, the report had a very positive effect: the marketing department suggested that the number of "positive impressions" the report generated may have equaled the equivalent of two Super Bowl advertising campaigns. The report also served as a "call to action" for others in the industry.

Monica eventually left Gap to run corporate responsibility and international trade at American Eagle Outfitters, and now heads corporate compliance for New Balance.

Later in Life

Others became Corporate Idealists later in their career. John Sherman had worked for a multinational utility for twenty-two years when his phone rang on January 2, 2001. There was an explosion at one of its facilities; three employees were engulfed in flames. One passed away after a few days and the other two survived.

As one of the company's head lawyers, John was responsible for defending the case. It went to mediation, and John was startled by his own reaction facing the two daughters of the deceased employee.

"The only thing I could think of doing was tell them how honored I was to be in their presence and how profoundly sorry I was," John told me. "One of his girls started to cry, and I have two girls of my own. It profoundly affected me." That was the turning point for John. He was a self-proclaimed "child of the late '60s" whose wife had marched with Martin Luther King Jr. Like many idealists, when kids came along John's priorities changed, and he went into law and a stable company job. Two decades later, this tragic accident brought out the activist in John that had been dormant for so long.

He began to research what other companies were doing on social responsibility, and in 2005 seized the opportunity to represent his company in the Business Leaders Initiative on Human Rights (BLIHR). Modeled on the Business Leaders Initiative on Climate Change, BLIHR brought together a dozen companies from different industries for quarterly discussions about human rights, often with external experts and activists. John became one of BLIHR's most active participants and champions. After he retired from the utility in 2008 he joined me on the team supporting the U.N. special representative on business and human rights. John had found his community, people like him who found themselves in corporate life and still wanted to do good in the world, which he called "liberating."

Dan Bross was leading State Government Affairs and

Community Affairs for a Fortune 500 oil and natural gas company in Houston when he had what he described to me as "the great awakening. Up to that point I was a gay man by night, and a buttoned-up corporate type by day. And ne'er the twain shall meet." In 1985, the city of Houston passed a nondiscrimination ordinance. He told me:

> The Houston Chamber of Commerce decided that this was the worst thing that could happen to Houston, that Houston would become Sodom and Gomorrah. I was sitting in the office of the chairman of this company, me in my three-piece suit and white shirt and red tie. They're talking about the activity by the Houston chamber to overturn this ordinance, and they're talking about the f-ing faggots and all the horrible sort of challenges that are going to befall the city of Houston.
>
> I was in charge of political giving, and I had to leave that meeting and go write a check for whatever it was, $30,000 or $50,000, to overturn this action by the Houston City Council. And that's when I decided that I could not do this. As a result of that, I knew that I had an incredibly compelling need to be who I was regardless if I was sitting in my office or if I was home on a weekend.

That night he began campaigning in support of the ordinance to counteract the work he was doing by day. As he later told a gathering of Lambda Legal, the national legal organization that works on behalf of lesbians, gay men, bisexuals, transgender people, and those with HIV: "I had to defeat that person I had become."

Dan left within a few months for a job more consistent with

his values, campaigning against a ballot initiative to require HIV testing for all California residents, then running the AIDS Action Council in D.C. Burnt out after five years of intense activist work, he took a job with a boutique lobbying firm; soon his main client, Microsoft, asked him to come on board. I asked Dan whether he had any qualms about rejoining corporate America after his Houston experience: "Quite the contrary. The fact that I could go to work for a company whose insurance would cover my partner, the fact that they would assist Bob in finding a job when we moved to Seattle from Washington, D.C.—it was a completely different experience and a reintroduction to a different part of corporate America."

He framed his job at the time as reintroducing Microsoft to regulators and opinion makers who only thought of the company as an aggressive monopolist. I challenged him on whether his job was just public relations, and he replied: "I think it originally started out as spin. And I can honestly say that I had some concern about that. But as we had more of these conversations, what we came to realize was spin could only get us so far: what we really needed to do was take a serious look at our policies and practices." Now, as Microsoft's director of corporate citizenship, Dan led the development of the Microsoft Global Human Rights Statement and works with business units across the company to embed responsible practices.

Serendipity... Sort Of

Other Corporate Idealists attribute their jobs to serendipity. After following her boyfriend to San Francisco with an international affairs degree but no job, Laura Rubbo landed a two-week temp position as an administrative assistant to the senior vice president of sourcing at Gap Inc., just as he was considering a new code of conduct for Gap suppliers. She ended up staying there for seven years and is now a senior director in the International Labor Standards department at Disney. Paul Ellingstad kept his passion for social justice outside of his job in marketing at HP until a woman who'd known him for ten years took over the social innovation department and asked him to join her. Of course, these opportunities weren't truly random—like I was when I joined BP, Laura and Paul were clear with themselves and vocal to others about where their true interests lay—but they hadn't directly pursued a Corporate Idealist job.

A Sorting Function

All of these Corporate Idealists have stories that are unique in their details but not in their themes. All of us wanted to make a positive difference in the world, and through a combination of searching and happenstance found our way into these roles.

Not everyone identifies as an idealist. As Ed Potter from The Coca-Cola Company put it, "Because if you're an idealist, you're not going to change your vector to accommodate a business. I view myself as a corporate NGO, the in-house NGO." Elliot Schrage from Facebook announced to me, "I'm a revolutionary incrementalist!" Dan Bross from Microsoft calls himself a "diplomatic agitator."

A number of people I spoke with preferred to describe themselves as pragmatic. One example is Jonathan Drimmer, vice president and assistant general counsel for Canadian mining company Barrick Gold, who joined the company in 2011 to implement a new human rights compliance program. Jonathan explained how, like his job now, his previous role investigating and prosecuting war crimes at the U.S. Department of Justice demanded practicality, even as the work was underpinned by morality:

> We would have people that we knew were guilty, absolutely knew up and down 100 percent guilty. Could we prove it? Probably. Could we prove it without question, beyond a reasonable doubt, and were we convinced that a court would find the same way we did? If the answer was no, we wouldn't bring the case. Yes, the person gets away, but you'll get the next one. So it is a strong sense of ethics, a strong sense of morals but there is also practicality. I don't want to charge somebody with war crimes and have them be acquitted. Idealistic? No. But a strong sense of ethics, and practical.

With all due respect to my practical friends, I still count them among my Corporate Idealist tribe. I do see idealism in their work, as much as they may want to frame it in other terms. Judy Samuelson, founder and head of the Aspen Institute's Business and Society Program, once led a group of business leaders through a set of pessimistic scenarios for the future, hoping to scare them into taking sustainability more seriously. It backfired: "Too dark," one of the participants grumbled at her. She told me:

> Those of us who end up in nonprofits tend to look at the world in a different way than people who go into business. I love working with business executives in part because they are all about opportunity; their glass truly is half full. You can't make a buck if you are mired

in doom and gloom. Many of us who work for non-profits are motivated by concern for the commons, but often the people motivated by the opportunity are the ones who see a way forward—the ones convinced there must be a solution.

Mila Rosenthal, formerly of Amnesty International USA and Human Rights Watch, actually believes that activists are relentlessly optimistic as well:

> You can't be an NGO idealist any more than you can a Corporate Idealist unless you're fundamentally extremely optimistic. Because otherwise you'd just slit your own throat, I mean, how do you get out of bed every morning and face this?! I think of that as a great quality of all the best advocates I've ever known: being very clear-eyed about the abuses in the world but being very strong in the belief that what you're doing can eventually make them better.

Meg Roggensack, who was an international trade attorney with a major law firm before working for Human Rights First, notes the "can-do" attitude of the companies she has engaged:

> Whether it's a law, rule, voluntary goal—companies just want to know what it is, and they can organize to deliver to that. We may have differences about what exactly they can do and how fast they can do it, and that's what we argue about. Where there isn't a clear commitment or standard, it's far more difficult. But business is structured to deliver: that's what they do and

they do that well. So where there is shared understanding, we can leverage business's core strengths to achieve our shared goals.

A number of Corporate Idealists expressed that bias toward optimism, opportunity, and action—not just to make a buck, but to make a difference. Even in the face of the disillusionment Jeffrey Hollender experienced in leaving Seventh Generation, he told me, "I get my optimism from knowing that change is possible and knowing that we have much of the capability and technology we need to deal with the challenges that are facing us."

Marcus Chung told me that he was visiting Gap Inc. suppliers in India when the person leading his trip took him to see a factory that was not Gap-approved:

It was in the middle of Delhi, in a highly populated urban area. It was a tiny little factory, one room on one floor of a multistory building, and I think there were apartments right next door and below and above it. The factory was producing goods for the domestic market, so no major brands were sourcing from it; it was producing woven shirts and probably had fifteen sewing machines. It was tiny, not a factory by any standard that we had worked with.

We walked in and the conditions were just abhorrent. It was dirty, it was tiny, there was garbage everywhere, the machines were really ancient and there were no safety mechanisms on any of them; the pulleys were all exposed. The most shocking thing was I saw a kid who was probably ten years old working on one of the machines. I thought, this is so different from the factory we had just visited.

But far from being discouraged by witnessing that scene, Marcus was optimistic:

It was actually one of the moments where I felt like all of this work that the brands are putting into compliance, into auditing, into working with factories, has elevated the type of factory that exports. But it opened my eyes to the whole other problem that I don't know what to do about, where you don't have export factories, where they're producing for domestic markets. This happens in every single country. The companies, the brands that are selling these products don't have the same standards or don't have the same expectations. The price points are so much lower that it's a whole other world; it's such a vast difference between the factories that I saw there versus the ones that I see on a daily basis.

It was heartening to think, this is probably where some factories were twenty, thirty years ago. Sometimes it feels like we're not making much progress, but we probably have if this was a typical factory otherwise.

We all struggle with what has happened in the time that we've been in these roles; there's so much more that needs to happen still. But it was a good touchpoint for me to realize that it feels like we've come a long way in the past few decades.

When Jonathan Drimmer of Barrick Gold first visited Papua New Guinea with the company, he learned about the extent of domestic violence there. Instead of being overwhelmed or dismissing the issue as irrelevant to the business, Jonathan saw an opportunity to help:

I felt like this is really going to be good human rights work. This is where a company really should be able to make a difference: through employment opportunities, through education programs, through supporting civil society groups, through working with government to educate the police about domestic violence and establish a family court. It became very clear that there were things we could do and ought to do.

The resource curse literature suggests that companies can exacerbate or create social problems, so funding educational programs might seem like the least a company could do. But as Jonathan points out and my experience with BP illustrated, a company is only one of many forces in a society. I wondered aloud to Jonathan whether Barrick made domestic violence worse by giving men jobs and money that put them in positions of even greater power; he said he learned that men who don't have jobs are around the house more, feel that their manhood is challenged, and consequently fight with women over how to spend their limited resources. "More like it shifts around what triggers violence. In communities where domestic violence is prevalent, jobs and money are neither the single cause nor the solution." He echoed the acceptance of incrementalism that I heard from other Corporate Idealists: "Anyone who enters into this work should know that you're never going to fully solve problems, especially social or community-based problems where multiple factors are at play. You can mitigate, you can seek positive approaches, you can take affirmative steps to try to make things better."

After I visited BP's Tangguh project in Indonesia for the first time, I accepted that the development was inevitable. Local people wanted the company there for the jobs and infrastructure; the government wanted us for the revenue; and global consumers needed the energy. So I thought of my mission as mitigating the risks and enhancing the benefits to communities as best we could. I also took comfort and pride in the fact that I was there specifically to mitigate those risks and enhance those benefits, whereas another company might not have had anyone doing so.

In 2002, under pressure from human rights groups, Talisman Energy exited an oil project in Sudan. ONGC, India's state oil and gas company, bought Talisman's stake—and ended communications with activists concerned about the region and the community programs that Talisman established. Some activists declared victory with Talisman's departure, but oil production increased and the people of Sudan may be no better off.

The Corporate Idealist community sees both the challenges and the potential of big business. We realize that we can't save the world—we can't even save every finger and toe. We can expound upon but not fully explain the disasters of our companies and industries, which is deeply unsatisfying to those who want simple answers and assurances. But we can nudge our companies toward a vision of a better future, one in which "responsible business" and "fair trade" are redundant, not novelties or oxymorons.

After working around the world for BP and the U.N. mandate, and a few years after that questioning whether any of it was worthwhile and where my heart and mind should be, I've arrived back home: in my hometown, with my family, and in the professional community where I belong.

The honeymoon is over for my love affair with the private sector. It is time to settle in for the long haul, recognizing that my partner isn't perfect and loving him all the more for it. Despite the failings of big business, I find myself still optimistic about its ability to make a positive difference in the world. I cheer small wins and incremental steps, and through crises see opportunities to bring about change. I am no longer that girl who fell in love with Big Oil fifteen years ago. But I must still be a Corporate Idealist.

Epilogue

MANIFESTO FOR THE CORPORATE IDEALIST

1. What is good for society is good for my company.
2. "Responsible business" should be redundant.
3. Sharing the stories of the people and communities my company affects is part of my job.
4. Evangelizing to my colleagues is not helpful. Figuring out how my work supports theirs is.
5. The "business case" is important. So is morality.
6. Leadership transitions and financial downturns are irrelevant if I've truly embedded my work.
7. All human rights are relevant to my company.
8. If consultation and collaboration aren't both frustrating and worthwhile, I'm not doing it right.
9. Transformational change is needed. Incremental change is good too.
10. The challenges we face are systemic and complex. But that doesn't mean I can't do anything about them.

Endnotes

Prologue

xv   **John Browne, chief executive of what was then British Petroleum, came to deliver a speech:** John Browne, "Leading a Global Company: The Case of BP," speech delivered at Yale University, September 18, 2000. Covered in Daniel P. Jones, "BP Breaks Ranks with Vow to Cut Greenhouse Gases," *The Courant*, September 19, 1998.

xv   **He had recently broken ranks:** John Browne, "Addressing Climate Change," speech delivered at Stanford University, May 19, 1997. Discussed in Darcy Frey, "How Green Is BP?" *The New York Times*, December 08, 2002.

xvi   **My parents both worked "in business":** Now I'm duly impressed with my parents' careers: my mother was in Human Resources for various banks then eventually retiring from the University of Pennsylvania, much to the dismay of Penn faculty who loved her ability to explain their benefits to them and advocate on their behalf. My father retired as an actuary, having written several papers explaining the many ways in which pension funds are mismanaged, years before the issue got on the national agenda with the 2009 collapse of General Motors and numerous state budgets due to their pension costs.

xviii   **deemphasized the progressive stances:** Shanta Barley, "BP Brings 'Green Era' to a Close," BBC News, May 11, 2009.

xviii   **"like a laser":** Terry Macalister, "Safety Failures and Delays Force BP to Slash Targets," *The Guardian*, February 6, 2007.

xviii   **the bad BP had been there all along:** See, for example, Jad Mouawad, "For BP, a History of Spills and Safety Lapses," *The New*

York Times, May 8, 2010; and Sarah Lyall, "In BP's Record, a History of Boldness and Costly Blunders," *The New York Times,* July 12, 2010.

xx **corporate social responsibility (CSR) and sustainability:** For the most part I use "corporate social responsibility," "corporate responsibility," "CSR," and "sustainability" interchangeably, to mean a company's impacts on people and the environment.

xx **mentioned in academic literature in the 1930s and '40s:** Archie Carroll, "Corporate Social Responsibility: Evolution of a Definitional Construct," *Business & Society,* Vol. 38 No. 3, September 1999: 268–295.

xx **more than half of the companies in the Fortune 500 published annual CSR or sustainability reports:** Governance & Accountability Institute, "Number of Companies in S&P 500 and Fortune 500 Reporting on Sustainability More Than Doubles from Previous Year," December 17, 2011.

Chapter 1: Indonesia

2 **enough to meet U.S. demand for natural gas for nearly eight months:** At 2001 consumption rates. *BP Statistical Review of World Energy 2013.*

2 **Papua:** Thanks to Kevin O'Rourke, my former colleague on BP's Tangguh project and author of *Reformasi: The Struggle for Power in Post-Soeharto Indonesia* (Allen & Unwin, 2002), for serving as a resource on Indonesian history and culture. Two informative reports on Papua, focused on political issues but including history and context, were produced by the Council on Foreign Relations: David L. Phillips (Project Director) and Dennis C. Blair (Chair), *Indonesia Commission: Peace and Progress in Papua,* 2003; and Blair A. King, *Peace in Papua: Widening a Window of Opportunity,* 2006.

3 **New Guinea is a biodiversity hotspot:** WWF, "New Guinea," wwf.panda.org.

3 **a new tribe being "discovered":** Reuters, "Indonesia Census Turns Up Papua Tribe Living in Trees," June 25, 2010.

3 **a name that locals never accepted but retained some official legal status:** Papua was split into two provinces in 2003, one of which was called "West Irian Jaya" until 2007.

4 **the "resource curse":** See, for example, Frederick van der Ploeg, "Natural Resources: Curse or Blessing?" *Journal of Economic Literature,* 49(2), 2011: 366–420.

5 **eleven Acehnese filed suit:** *John Doe I et. al. v. ExxonMobil Corporation et. al.,* Complaint filed in the U.S. District Court for the District of

Columbia, June 11, 2001, available with other relevant documentation at Business & Human Rights Resource Centre, "Case profile: ExxonMobil Lawsuit (re Aceh)," business-humanrights.org. The case was expected to be dismissed after the 2013 U.S. Supreme Court ruling in *Kiobel v. Royal Dutch Petroleum* that foreign plaintiffs may not sue corporations in U.S. courts for human rights violations committed abroad. See, for example, Ian T. Shearn and Laird Townsend, "Did ExxonMobil Pay Torturers?" *Mother Jones,* October 5, 2012; and Steve Coll, *Private Empire: ExxonMobil and American Power* (New York: The Penguin Press, 2012), 120.

6   **in a speech at Stanford University:** Browne, "Addressing Climate Change."

7   **in the speech I attended at Yale:** Browne, "Leading a Global Company: The Case of BP."

7   **"suggest heat, light, and nature":** BP, "Our logo," bp.com.

7   **"Most Admired Leader":** 1999–2001: Chris Blackhurst, "2001: Britain's Most Admired Companies," *Management Today,* December 1, 2001. 2002: Andrew Saunders, "Britain's Most Admired Companies: Double First," *Management Today,* December 1, 2002.

7   **"not victory or conquest":** John Browne, "The Case for Social Responsibility," speech delivered at Business for Social Responsibility's annual conference, Boston, November 10, 1998.

7   **Colombia was BP's first foray:** John Browne, *Beyond Business,* (London: Weidenfeld & Nicolson, 2010), 90–109; Jenny Pearce, *Beyond the Perimeter Fence: Oil and Armed Conflict in Casanare, Colombia,* Centre for the Study of Global Governance, February 26, 2009; and BP, "A security and human rights legacy in Colombia," bp.com.

8   **"Leaders are not perfect":** John Browne, *Beyond Business,* 107.

16   **Kathie Lee Gifford would cry:** Charles Bowden, "Charlie Kernaghan, Keeper of the Fire," *Mother Jones,* July/August 2003.

16   **Phil Knight would admit that his company, Nike:** Phil Knight, speech delivered at the National Press Club, May 12, 1998; covered in John H. Cushman Jr., "Nike Pledges to End Child Labor and Apply U.S. Rules Abroad," *The New York Times,* May 13, 1998.

20   **Major General Mahidin Simbolon:** Abdul Khalik, "CTF Implicates Generals in 1999 East Timor Violence," *The Jakarta Post,* July 16, 2008; and Human Rights Watch, "Justice Denied for East Timor," December 20, 2002.

20   **the Ken Saro-Wiwa case:** See, for example, Jad Mouawad, "Oil Industry Braces for Trial on Rights Abuses," *The New York Times,* May 21, 2009; and Elizabeth Neuffer, "Big Oil and an Activist's Death," *Boston*

Globe, June 3, 2001. Extensive documentation and commentary on the Ken Saro-Wiwa case available at Business and Human Rights Resource Centre, "Case Profile: Shell Lawsuit (Re Nigeria)," business-humanrights.org.

20 **"It is not for commercial organizations like Shell..."**: Paul Lewis, "After Nigeria Represses, Shell Defends Its Record," *The New York Times,* February 13, 1996.

24 **Global Witness put out a press release:** Global Witness, "Campaign Success: BP Makes Move for Transparency in Angola," February 12, 2001. Episode described and Sonangol letter excerpted in John Browne, *Beyond Business,* 113–119 and Human Rights Watch, *Some Transparency, No Accountability: The Use of Oil Revenue in Angola and Its Impact on Human Rights,* January 2004.

27 **seven members of the army's special forces:** Richard C. Paddock, "7 Convicted in Assassination of Papuan Separatist Leader," *Los Angeles Times,* April 22, 2003.

28 **Some of the companies privately fought government requests:** See, for example, Claire Cain Miller, "Secret Court Ruling Put Tech Companies in Data Bind," *The New York Times,* June 13, 2013.

30 **As Chris Avery, founder of the Business and Human Rights Resource Centre, has written:** Chris Avery, "The difference between CSR and human rights," Corporate Citizenship Briefing, August/September 2006.

32 **We published the two and a half pages of bullet points:** Gare A. Smith and Bennett Freeman, *Human Rights Assessment of the Proposed Tangguh LNG Project: Summary of Recommendations and Conclusion,* April 19, 2002, available at BP Indonesia, "Human Rights and Tangguh," bp.com.

33 **the human rights impact assessment proved useful for Tangguh, but also turned out to be a model:** See, for example, Business and Human Rights Resource Centre, "Human Rights Impact and Compliance Assessments," business-humanrights.org.

33 **Yahoo! conducted a human rights impact assessment:** Douglas MacMillan, "Yahoo's Bold Advance into the Middle East," *BloombergBusinessWeek,* August 26, 2009, in particular the following quote: "Yahoo Deputy General Counsel Michael Samway says when the company was performing its due diligence, it studied 'the potential intersection points with human-rights challenges.'" See also Yahoo!, Business and Human Rights Program, "Human Rights Impact Assessments," www.yhumanrightsblog.com.

34 **ExxonMobil's 2001 four-month shutdown:** Cost of $350.8 million cited in "Gas Flows Again from ExxonMobil's Arun Fields," *The*

Jakarta Post, July 29, 2001. Estimate of $300 million to $500 million *annual* net income in Michael Schuman and Thaddeus Herrick, "Exxon Mobil's Gas Shutdown In Aceh Shows Unrest's Cost," *The Wall Street Journal,* April 4, 2001. Annual profits of $498 million cited in Steve Coll, *Private Empire: ExxonMobil and American Power,* 95.

34 **A *Forbes* article said that Freeport spent $28 million:** Simon Montlake, "Cave In: Freeport-McMoRan Digs a Heap of Trouble in Indonesia," *Forbes Magazine,* February 13, 2012.

35 **as a green buffer zone:** Tangguh Independent Advisory Panel, *Fourth Report on Tangguh LNG Project,* March 2006, 3 (footnote 7).

36 **a *Wall Street Journal* reporter:** Timothy Mapes, "For BP to Gain in Irian Jaya, the Locals Must Benefit, Too," *The Wall Street Journal,* November 15, 2001.

36 **the *Economist* wrote:** "BP in Indonesia: Sociologists Before Geologists?," *The Economist,* June 27, 2002.

39 **a 1997 measles epidemic:** Mapes, "For BP to Gain in Irian Jaya, the Locals Must Benefit, Too"; and Smith and Freeman, *Human Rights Assessment of the Proposed Tangguh LNG Project.*

39 **allegations of corruption among the third-party recruiters BP had hired:** Michael M. Cernea, *BP Tangguh LNG Project: LARAP's Implementation Performance in 2006: 2nd Report of the External Monitoring Panel,* May 15, 2007, 47.

41 **The panel's final report in 2009:** Tangguh Independent Advisory Panel, *Seventh Report on the Tangguh LNG Project,* March 2009, available at BP Indonesia, "TIAP Reports and BP Responses," bp.com. After Tangguh's construction, BP established a new advisory panel for the project's operations phase. The Asian Development Bank has also monitored the social and environmental aspects of the Tangguh LNG project, with all reports available at adb.org.

42 **in a phrase sprinkled liberally in company statements and literature:** Most notably in the 2002 "What We Stand For," the company's statement of business policies; and, for example, BP New Zealand, *2002 Triple Bottom Line Report*; and Simon Montlake, "A Test for Big Oil in Indonesia," *The Christian Science Monitor,* May 21, 2002.

Chapter 2: China

45 **In 2003 China reported some seven hundred thousand serious work-related accidents and one hundred thirty thousand fatalities:** John Bellamy Foster and Robert W. McChesney, *The Endless*

Crisis: How Monopoly-Finance Capital Produces Stagnation and Upheaval from the U.S.A. to China (New York: Monthly Review Press, 2012), 175.

47 **Papua New Guinea, where domestic violence is reported to affect two-thirds of all families:** ChildFund Australia, *Stop Violence Against Women and Children in Papua New Guinea,* August 2013.

49 **no real unions:** The All-China Federation of Trade Unions, China's sole union, is "essentially made toothless and discredited by the contradictions of its role as both a defender of labor and a government institution." Alexandra Harney, *The China Price: The True Cost of Chinese Competitive Advantage* (New York: The Penguin Press, 2008), 131.

51 **Mark Nordstrom, Senior Labor and Employment Counsel for GE, who attended the conference, wrote in a blog post:** Mark Nordstrom, "China and Human Rights," May 3, 2013, www.gecitizenship.com.

52 **John Elkington... wrote in a *New York Times* op-ed:** John Elkington, "Going Green," *The New York Times,* June 21, 2012.

58 **then-CEO Phil Knight said:** Phil Knight, speech at the National Press Club, May 12, 1998.

58 **a *New York Times* exposé:** Charles Duhigg and David Barboza, "In China, Human Costs Are Built Into an iPad," *The New York Times,* January 25, 2012.

66 **Shenzhen and Shanghai Stock Exchanges:** "Shenzhen Stock Exchange Social Responsibility Instructions to Listed Companies," September 25, 2006, www.szse.cn. "SSE [Shanghai Stock Exchange] Drives Listed Companies to Fulfill Social Responsibilities," May 14, 2008, english.sse.com.cn. Covered in World Federation of Exchanges, "Raising CSR Standards and Disclosure Practices," August 2009, www.world-exchanges.org.

68 **In response to unrest around major projects both at home and abroad:** See, for example, Shapi Shacinda, "Workers Shot During Zambia Mine Riots," *Mail & Guardian,* July 26, 2006; and Barry Bearak, "Zambia Uneasily Balances Chinese Investment and Workers' Resentment," *The New York Times,* November 20, 2010.

68 **partnerships with the British and Swedish governments:** The Embassy of Sweden in Beijing, "Corporate Social Responsibility in China," www.swedenabroad.com; China CSR Map, "UK Department for International Development China," www.chinacsrmap.org.

68 **In 2012, China's State Council ordered:** See, for example, James A. Kent, "The Social Risk: When Citizens Organize to Fight a Project," EnergyBiz.com, Aug 20, 2013; and Keith Bradsher, "'Social Risk' Test Ordered by China for Big Projects," *The New York Times,* November 12, 2012.

70 **Sir Geoffrey Chandler:** "Challenges of Globalisation: The Flaw of the 'Business Case'," speech delivered at the Environment Foundation's Windsor Consultation at St. George's House, Windsor Castle, December 12, 2001.

Chapter 3: London

74 **ExxonMobil's four-month shutdown:** As noted in chapter 1, estimates from "Gas Flows Again from ExxonMobil's Arun Fields," *The Jakarta Post*; Schuman and Herrick, "Exxon Mobil's Gas Shutdown In Aceh Shows Unrest's Cost"; and Coll, *Private Empire.*

75 **the International Finance Corporation began developing a tool:** International Financial Corporation, "Financial Valuation Tool for Sustainability Investments," www.fvtool.com.

76 **Capital expenditure:** *BP Annual Report and Accounts 2005,* 12.

82 **BP "has not adequately established process safety as a core value across all its five U.S. refineries":** James A. Baker, III, *et. al., The Report of the B.P. U.S. Refineries Independent Safety Review Panel,* January 2007, xii.

83 **Marci, a community affairs liaison:** The names of the staff in the Indonesia workshop have been changed.

86 **As Chris Avery, founder of the Business and Human Rights Resource Centre, has written:** Avery, "The Difference Between CSR and Human Rights."

86 **Four days before the 2005 opening ceremony of BP's Baku–Tblisi–Ceyhan pipeline:** Tim Wall, "A Social Explosion in the Pipeline," *The Moscow Times,* June 7, 2005.

87 **the *Economist* suggested:** "The Oil Satrap: David Woodward and Being a Giant in a Small Country," *The Economist,* June 9, 2005.

88 **a similar document from the mining company Rio Tinto:** Rio Tinto, "Human Rights Guidance," October 2003, www.riotinto.com.

88 **The note went up on bp.com:** The 2006 BP human rights guidance note was replaced by a new Human Rights Policy, posted on bp.com in 2013.

90 **Even prior to the Texas City refinery explosion in 2005 BP had begun reviewing all policies:** At a press conference on January 16, 2007, following the publication of the Baker Panel Report, John Browne said: "The actions we are taking date back not only to the Texas City accident in 2005, but some date back to 2003 when we embarked on a major journey to strengthen our operations and system of internal control, following the growth in scale of the group." Available at www.investor-claims-against-bp.com (accessed September 30, 2013).

90 **the 2008 launch of a new operating management system:** BP, "How We Operate," bp.com.

92 **"identify and clarify standards of corporate responsibility":** Office of the High Commissioner for Human Rights, "Human Rights and Transnational Corporations and Other Business Enterprises," Human Rights Resolution 2005/69 (E-CN_4-RES-2005-69), April 20, 2005.

95 **he responded in an open letter:** John Ruggie, "Re: Joint NGO Response to Interim Report," Letter, May 22, 2006, available at business-humanrights.org.

95 **The NGO Global Witness:** Global Witness, "UN/SRSG & Global Witness Team Up," Press Release, October 3, 2007. See, for example, Seema Joshi, *Business & Human Rights in Conflict Zones: The Role of Home States,* November 5, 2007, available at business-humanrights.org.

98 **Browne later wrote in his autobiography:** Browne, *Beyond Business,* 215.

100 **Hayward stated his intentions:** Barley, "BP Brings 'Green Era' to a Close."

100 **Hayward explained his approach:** Tony Hayward, "Entrepreneurial Spirit Needed," speech given at Stanford Business School, May 12, 2009.

101 **"shareholder value is not about returns and growth rates alone":** Browne, *Beyond Business,* 231.

102 **in May 2012 he gave his first public talk:** Arup, "Lord Browne Addresses Connect Out," Arup.com, May 29, 2012.

102 **he wrote an op-ed in the *Financial Times*:** John Browne, "Three Reasons Why I'm Voting for Gay Marriage," *Financial Times,* June 2, 2013.

102 *The Glass Closet*: Charlotte Williams, "WH Allen Buys *Glass Closet* from Browne," June 11, 2013, www.thebookseller.com.

Chapter 4: The United Nations

In addition to the links below, sources in this chapter related to the U.N. special representative on business and human rights can be found at the Business and Human Rights Resource Centre, "U.N. Special Representative," business-humanrights.org.

106 **In 2001, the United Steelworkers Union and the International Labor Rights Fund filed suit:** Business and Human Rights Resource Centre, Corporate Legal Accountability Portal, "Case Profile: Coca-Cola Lawsuit (Re Colombia)," business-humanrights .org.

111 **the U.N. Commission on Transnational Corporations:** For an overview of the U.N.'s history on this topic see Giovanni Mantilla, "Emerging International Human Rights Norms for Transnational Corporations," *Global Governance* 15 (2009): 279–298.

112 ***Draft Norms on the Responsibilities of Transnational Corporations and Other Business Enterprises with Regard to Human Rights:*** *Draft Norms on the Responsibilities of Transnational Corporations and Other Business Enterprises with Regard to Human Rights,* E/CN.4/Sub.2/2003/12 (2003).

112 **The *Norms* provoked a strong negative reaction:** International Organisation of Employers and International Chamber of Commerce, *Joint Views of the IOE and ICC on the Draft Norms on the Responsibilities of Transnational Corporations and Other Business Enterprises with Regard to Human Rights,* March 2004, available at business-humanrights.org.

112 **BP's response to the commission's call for public input on the *Norms:*** Letter from Graham Baxter, BP, to Dzidek Kedzia, Office of the High Commissioner for Human Rights, 1 October 2004, available at Office of the High Commissioner for Human Rights, "Stakeholder Submissions to the Report of the High Commissioner for Human Rights on the Responsibilities of Transnational Corporations and Related Business Enterprises with Regard to Human Rights," www.ohchr.org.

113 **the *Norms* should "be used as the main basis":** Amnesty International, "Submission by Amnesty International under Decision 2004/116 on the "Responsibilities of Transnational Corporations and Related Business Enterprises with Regard to Human Rights," September 2004, also available at www.ohchr.org.

113 **In 2004 the Commission on Human Rights declined to consider the *Norms:*** Commission on Human Rights, Decision 2004/116, "Responsibilities of Transnational Corporations and Related Business Enterprises with regard to Human Rights," April 20, 2004.

113 **The Commission on Human Rights passed a resolution:** Commission on Human Rights, Human Rights Resolution 2005/69, "Human Rights and Transnational Corporations and Other Business Enterprises," April 20, 2005.

114 **John partnered with the Business and Human Rights Resource Centre:** Business and Human Rights Resource Centre, "U.N. Special Representative," business-humanrights.org.

115 **I drafted discussion papers:** *Reporting on non-financial performance, Revenue Sharing and Fiscal Management, Security of People and Assets,* and

Human Rights Impact Assessments, all available at Business and Human Rights Resource Centre, business-humanrights.org.

116 **In his 2008 report to the Human Rights Council:** *Protect, Respect and Remedy: a Framework for Business and Human Rights,* A/HRC/8/5, April 7, 2008.

117 **In his 2006 report to the Human Rights Council:** John Ruggie, *Interim Report of the Special Representative of the Secretary-General on the Issue of Human Rights and Transnational Corporations and Other Business Enterprises,* U.N. Doc. E/CN.4/2006/97 (2006), February 2006.

118 **"They don't listen to us":** John Gerard Ruggie, *Just Business: Multinational Corporations and Human Rights* (New York: W.W. Norton & Company, 2013), xli.

118 **The "Protect, Respect and Remedy" framework was welcomed by the Human Rights Council:** Human Rights Council Resolution 8/7, "Mandate of the Special Representative of the Secretary-General on the Issue of Human Rights and Transnational Corporations and Other Business Enterprises," June 18, 2008.

119 **"Students of international law and regulatory policy...":** Ruggie, *Just Business,* 144.

119 **a wide variety of organizations started using the "Protect, Respect and Remedy" framework:** Examples compiled in Special Representative of the United Nations Secretary-General for Business and Human Rights *Applications of the U.N. 'Protect, Respect and Remedy' Framework,* June 30, 2011, available at business-humanrights.org.

120 **as John explained in presenting it to the council:** John Ruggie, "Presentation of Report to United Nations Human Rights Council," June 3, 2008, available at business-humanrights.org.

121 **the sustainability goals that Lee Scott announced for Walmart in 2005:** Lee Scott, "Twenty First Century Leadership," October 24, 2005.

122 **"If it's about your mission...":** Seth Godin, *Tribes: We Need You to Lead Us* (New York: Portfolio, 2008), 136.

125 **a satirical 2009 video by *The Onion*:** The Onion, "Ambassador Stages Coup At U.N., Issues Long List of Non-Binding Resolutions," theonion.com.

128 **subsequent news stories:** See, for example, Mouawad, "For BP, a History of Spills and Safety Lapses" and Lyall, "In BP's Record, a History of Boldness and Costly Blunders."

128 **President Obama even chided the company's "recklessness":** The White House, "Remarks by the President to the Nation on the BP Oil Spill," June 15, 2010, www.whitehouse.gov.

128 **John Ruggie delivered a lecture at the Royal Society of Arts:** Sir Geoffrey Chandler Speaker Series, January 11, 2011, available at business-humanrights.org.

129 **His speech was covered favorably:** Hugh Williamson, "Conflict Zone Pressure Rises on Companies," *Financial Times,* January 12, 2011.

129 **"Rights groups slam U.N. plan for multinationals":** Hugh Williamson, *Financial Times,* January 17, 2011.

129 **"strongly worded statement" by Amnesty International:** "Joint Civil Society Statement on the Draft Guiding Principles on Business and Human Rights," January 2011. Subsequent letters available at ft.com and business-humanrights.org.

131 **John woke up to a memo in his inbox written by Martin Lipton:** Memos from Lipton and Milstein described and available at Michael D. Goldhaber, "A Sarbanes-Oxley for Human Rights?' *The AmLaw Daily,* June 2, 2008. Lipton's subsequent endorsement of the Guiding Principles described and available at Michael D. Goldhaber, "The Global Lawyer: Marty Likes It," December 20, 2010.

132 **We got statements from...:** Available at Business and Human Rights Resource Centre, business-humanrights.org.

134 **Enron had a Code of Ethics:** "Enron's 'Code Of Ethics,'" thesmokinggun.com.

135 **Norway and Argentina spoke first:** Summary of statements at Human Rights Council, "Council Establishes Working Group on Human Rights and Transnational Corporations and Other Business Enterprises," June 16, 2011, ohchr.org. Video archive at U.N. Human Rights Council Archived Video, Human Rights Council Seventeenth Session, un.org.

135 **Daniel Baer, deputy assistant secretary of state for Democracy, Human Rights and Labor, said:** "Businesses and Transnational Corporations Have a Responsibility to Respect Human Rights," June 16, 2011, www.humanrights.gov.

138 **the 2010 video clip of China's delegation:** U.N. Human Rights Council Archived Video, Human Rights Council Fourteenth Session, un.org.

138 **the U.S. State Department issued reporting requirements:** U.S. Department of State and U.S. Department of the Treasury, "Administration Eases Financial and Investment Sanctions on Burma," May 23, 2013, humanrights.gov.

139 **Secretary of State Hillary Clinton referenced the Guiding Principles and John Ruggie:** Hillary Rodham Clinton, Commemoration of the 50th Anniversary of the OECD on Guidelines for Multinational Enterprises, May 25, 2011, state.gov.

140 **Walmart has more than one hundred thousand suppliers:** "The Responsibility to Lead," talk at the Council on Foreign Relations (figure cited in introduction by Daniel L. Doctoroff), December 11, 2012, cfr.org.

141 **the five-person Working Group:** Office of the High Commissioner for Human Rights, "Working Group on the Issue of Human Rights and Transnational Corporations and Other Business Enterprises," ohchr.org.

Chapter 5: Gulf of Mexico

146 **"scathing portrait of cultural failure":** Mouawad, "For BP, a History of Spills and Safety Lapses."

146 **"managers had become deaf to risk":** Abrahm Lustgarten, "Furious Growth and Cost Cuts Led to BP Accidents Past and Present," ProPublica and PBS *Frontline*, October 26, 2010.

147 **ProPublica, the respected independent news organization, did a joint investigation with PBS *Frontline*:** Lustgarten, "Furious Growth and Cost Cuts Led to BP Accidents Past and Present," October 26, 2010.

147 **"These incidents and subsequent analyses":** National Commission on the BP Deepwater Horizon Oil Spill and Offshore Drilling, *Deep Water: The Gulf Oil Disaster and the Future of Offshore Drilling,* January 2011, Chapter 8, 218.

147 **"BP Group policies set high expectations":** National Commission on the BP Deepwater Horizon Oil Spill and Offshore Drilling, Chapter 8, 219.

147 **"There is a complete contradiction between BP's words and deeds":** Opening Statement of Representative Henry A. Waxman, Chairman, Committee on Energy and Commerce, The Role of BP in the Deepwater Horizon Explosion and Oil Spill, Subcommittee on Oversight and Investigations, June 17, 2010.

148 **"Senior management told us they are very serious about safety":** Lyall, "In BP's Record, a History of Boldness and Costly Blunders."

149 **"It's not unusual for a person...":** Peter Lattman, "An Ex-Trader, Now a Sociologist, Looks at the Changes in Goldman," *The New York Times,* September 30, 2013.

150 **Marcus Chung:** "A Report from Bangladesh," guest blog post on www.marcgunther.com, January 27, 2013.

151 **only eighteen labor inspectors:** Human Rights Watch, "Bangladesh: Tragedy Shows Urgency of Worker Protections," April 25, 2013.

151 **10 percent of the country's legislators own garment factories:** Jim Yardley, "Garment Trade Wields Power in Bangladesh," *The New York Times,* July 24, 2013.

151 **thirteen employees of Foxconn:** Business and Human Rights Resource Centre, "Foxconn Suicides—2010," business-humanrights.org.

153 *The China Price*: Harney, *The China Price:* 200, 203.

153 **"Overstretched suppliers..."**: Tom Idle, "Tesco CEO Admits That Era of Cheap Food Is Over—And That Suppliers Need Longer Contracts," July 22, 2013, 2degreesnetwork.com.

153 **Some companies like the Swedish clothing retailer H&M have stated their intent:** H&M, "Choose and Reward Responsible Partners," hm.com, as reported in Vikas Bajaj, "Doing Business in Bangladesh," *The New York Times,* September 14, 2013.

155 **"People change what they do..."**: John Kotter, *The Heart of Change* (Boston: Harvard Business School Press), 2002, 1. Emphasis in the original.

158 **"John Ruggie said it nicely in his book"**: "I will let my heart drive my commitment to human rights. But I'll need my head to steer the heart through the very difficult global terrain on which we are traveling." Ruggie, *Just Business,* 1.

160 **Ford came under fire:** Mark Dowie, "Pinto Madness," *Mother Jones,* September/October 1977.

160 **ExxonMobil's shutdown due to civil unrest in Aceh ($100 million to $350 million):** As noted in chapter 1, estimates from "Gas Flows Again from ExxonMobil's Arun Fields," *The Jakarta Post;* Schuman and Herrick, "Exxon Mobil's Gas Shutdown in Aceh Shows Unrest's Cost"; and Coll, *Private Empire.*

160 **Deepwater Horizon explosion ($42 billion and counting):** Margaret Cronin Fisk, Brian Swint, and Laurel Calkins, "BP's Oil Spill Deal Sours as Claims Add Billions to Cost," Bloomberg.com, June 5, 2013; and Stanley Reed, "Spill Claims Rising, BP Announces Weak Results," *The New York Times,* July 30, 2013.

160 **a major mine can lose $20 million:** Rachel Davis and Daniel M. Franks, *The Costs of Conflict with Local Communities in the Extractive*

Industry, presented at First Annual Seminar for Social Responsibility in Mining, 2011.

168 **Yahoo! demonstrated how to implement:** Yahoo! Business and Human Rights Program, yhumanrightsblog.com.

170 **ensuring good working conditions would add less than one dollar to the price of a pair of blue jeans:** Mehul Srivastava and Sarah Shannon, "Ninety Cents Buys Safety on $22 Jeans in Bangladesh," Bloomberg.com, June 6, 2013.

170 **only half of customers chose a pair of socks:** Howard Kimeldorf, Rachel Meyer, Monica Prasad, and Ian Robinson, "Consumers with a Conscience: Will They Pay More?" *Contexts,* February 2006, vol. 5: 124–29, as cited in Quentin Fottrell, "Would You Pay More for Fair-Trade Socks? Why Shoppers Don't Care About Bangladesh," MarketWatch, May 14, 2013.

172 **Kevin Hagen was corporate responsibility manager for REI:** Joel Makower, "Exit Interview: Kevin Hagen, REI," Greenbiz.com, April 24, 2013.

174 **BP's controversial attempts to publish its government payments in Angola helped bring about the Extractive Industries Transparency Initiative:** Extractive Industries Transparency Initiative, "History of EITI," eiti.org.

174 **BP's internal emissions trading program:** David G. Victor and Joshua C. House, "BP's Emissions Trading System," *Energy Policy* 34 (2006): 2100–2112.

176 **"that puts social values first":** Fairphone, fairphone.com.

178 **He said in a TED talk:** Dan Pallotta, "The Way We Think About Charity Is Dead Wrong," TED Talk, March 2013.

179 **"The angels don't need our help":** Ruggie, *Just Business,* 5.

179 **Bill McDonough wrote in *Cradle to Cradle*:** William McDonough and Michael Braungart, *Cradle to Cradle: Remaking the Way We Make Things* (New York: North Point Press, 2002), 149.

Chapter 6: New York City

187 **Tempered radicals:** Debra E. Meyerson, *Tempered Radicals: How People Use Difference to Inspire Change at Work,* (Boston: Harvard Business School Press, 2012): xi, 173 (emphasis in the original). Also see the article that preceded the book: Meyerson and Maureen A. Scully, "Tempered Radicalism and the Politics of Ambivalence and Change," *Organization Science,* Vol. 6, No. 5. (Sep.–Oct. 1995): 585–600.

188 **"Human beings can't help it"**: Godin, *Tribes,* 3.

197 **Gap published a CSR report:** Gap Inc., *2003 Social Responsibility Report*, gapinc.com.

197 **believed to be the first social responsibility report:** Patrick M. Wright, "Corporate Social Responsibility at Gap: An Interview with Eva Sage-Gavin," Cornell University, School of Industrial and Labor Relations, Center for Advanced Human Resource Studies, Working Paper #06–14, 2006.

197 **"risking unprecedented honesty in reporting":** *Corporate Responsibility Magazine,* "Business Ethics Annual Award Winners: 1989–2006," thecro.com.

197 **An article in the *MIT Sloan Management Review* said:** N. Craig Smith, Sean Ansett and Lior Erez, "How Gap Inc. Engaged with Its Stakeholders," *MIT Sloan Management Review,* Summer 2011. See also Simon English, "Gap Admits to Running Sweatshops," *The Telegraph,* May 13, 2004.

207 **Talisman Energy exited an oil project in Sudan:** Lison Joseph, "ONGC's Sudan Deals Come Under Attack," *Live Mint,* June 30, 2008; and Reg Manhas, "Talisman in Sudan: Impacts of Divestment," *Compact Quarterly,* March 2007.

Resources

Browne, John. *Beyond Business*. London: Weidenfeld & Nicolson, 2010.

Business and Human Rights Resource Centre, business -humanrights.org.

Freeman, Bennett and Gare A. Smith. *Human Rights Assessment of the Proposed Tangguh LNG Project: Summary of Recommendations and Conclusion*, April 19, 2002.

Global Network Initiative, globalnetworkinitiative.org.

Office of the United Nations High Commissioner for Human Rights, *et. al.*, *Human Rights Translated: A Business Reference Guide*, 2008.

Ruggie, John. *Guiding Principles on Business and Human Rights: Implementing the United Nations "Protect, Respect and Remedy" Framework*. A/HRC/17/31, March 21, 2011.

Ruggie, John. *Just Business: Multinational Corporations and Human Rights*. New York: W.W. Norton & Company, 2013.

Universal Declaration on Human Rights, un.org/en/ documents/udhr.

Voluntary Principles on Security & Human Rights, voluntary principles.org.

Acknowledgments

All of the idealists, pragmatists, cynics, advocates, and experts who shared their stories and thoughts with me, including those not named in these pages

Erika Heilman, Jill Friedlander, Shevaun Beltzer, Jill Schoenhaut, Susan Lauzau, and the Bibliomotion community

Jim Levine and Kerry Sparks at Levine Greenberg Literary Agency

My former BP colleagues for their counsel, recollections, and reflections

Team Ruggie

BSR, with special thanks to Faris Natour, Peter Nestor, Eva Dienel, and Aron Cramer, as well as the New York and Human Rights teams and the Human Rights Working Group

ACKNOWLEDGMENTS

Joanne Bauer and Zori Barkan at Columbia University

Noah Pickus and the Kenan Institute for
Ethics at Duke University

Nathaniel Stein for fact-checking and advice

The many friends, students, and peers who
reviewed drafts, including but not limited to Kevin
O'Rourke, Jenn Chen, Peter Stern, Angela Sapp
Mancini, Ward Duvall, Yousuf Aftab, Ariel
Meyerstein, Sarah Smith, Wendy Suzuki, Valerie Keller,
Elmira Bayrasli, and Becky Haldane

Heidi Brooks, Amy Wrzesniewski, and the Yale
School of Management

My writer role models and resources, espe-
cially Ron Lieber, Jodi Kantor, Kate Linebaugh,
Marci Alboher, Amy Whitaker, Katie Orenstein,
Cali Yost, Julie Burstein, and Jimmy Soni

Heidie, Steve, Dorian, Sharlene

Carrie, Mom, Stewart, Larry, Jeff, Ken, Peggy, Sam, Lexy

Alexander and Claire, for the inspiration and imperative to
work with purpose and pride

Adrian, for ev'rythin'.

Index

INDEX

INDEX

About the Author

Christine Bader is a lecturer and visiting scholar at Columbia University and a human rights advisor to BSR, the global business network focused on sustainability. She speaks, writes, and consults about corporate responsibility and sustainability, the intersection of business and human rights, and navigating careers with impact.

After earning her MBA from Yale she worked for BP in Indonesia, China, and the U.K., managing the social impacts of company projects in the developing world. In 2006 she created a part-time *pro bono* position as advisor to the United Nations secretary-general's special representative on business and human rights, a role she took up full-time from 2008-2011.

Christine has also served as a corps member with City Year, a teaching fellow in community service at Phillips Academy Andover, and special assistant to the New York City mayor's chief of staff and deputy mayor.

Christine played squash and rugby at Amherst College and competed in the 2002 World Ultimate Frisbee Club Championships, but now finds her athletic glory running along the Hudson River. She lives with her husband, son, and daughter in New York City.